Contents

KU-413-099

Acknowledgements

In preparing this edition the editor, although entirely responsible for the final selection, is grateful for the advice and help of Graham Owens and Andrew Best. A particular debt of gratitude is due to Michael Simpson, whose work in television drama for schools and whose knowledge of both schools and television was of great value in considering the plays to be included.

Anyone using material from the *Z Cars* series also owes a debt to those who initiated and coordinated the series. These include Troy Kennedy-Martin, who originated the idea and wrote the first scripts; Elwyn Jones, who was Head of Drama Series; John McGrath, who directed a number of the earlier episodes; and David E. Rose, who was the producer for the whole series.

M.M.

We are grateful to the following for permission to include those scripts which are in copyright. Applications for performance rights should be addressed to the authors' agents as below.

Keith Dewhurst, c/o Theatrework (London) Ltd, 22 Hans Road, London S.W.3. for *Running Milligan*;

Ronald Eyre, c/o Richard Hatton Ltd, 17a Curzon Street, London, W.1. for *Window Dressing*;

John Hopkins, c/o Richard Hatton Ltd, for *A Place of Safety*;

Alan Plater, c/o Margaret Ramsey Ltd, 14a Goodwins Court, London W.C.2. for *A Quiet Night*;

All the illustrations in this volume are from 'Tele-Snaps' by John Cura, 176a Northcote Road, London, S.W.11. We are grateful to him for permission to reproduce this copyright material.

'An introduction for Teachers' by Michael Marland is based on an article 'Z Cars and the Teacher' which was first published in *The Use of English* (Spring, 1967).

Thinking about Z Cars

These four scripts are not isolated works that happen to use common characters and be set in roughly the same area. They are plays written to commission. They belong to one of the most popular drama series on television. They have to be seen in this wide context—and that means looking at the whole of television and even beyond that to the facts of mid-twentieth-century English life.

What is television?

Television is no more than an electronic way of carrying words and pictures from one place to another. At its best it meets a need. For example, it can direct airline passengers to the right plane and keep them in touch with the life of an airport. It can bring to medical students a close-up picture of an operation that they could not otherwise see. It allows the police to observe traffic jams and plot ways out of them. It can help the teacher shortage by transmitting lessons and demonstrations from one school to another. To an audience that would not otherwise expect an invitation, it can bring great national events—like the funeral of a national leader. It can carry news that affects the whole nation: matters of peace and war and the Budget. Television is, in other words, a multi-purpose one-way visual telephone whose value to hospitals and schools and airports is obvious. It satisfies a need.

Who needs domestic television?

The television companies find themselves in possession of this elaborate, powerful, important instrument and note with alarm that television by its very nature is at its best in emergencies. Like a telephone it is valuable in moments of distress, elation and need. But imagine a situation in which you were required to talk, sing, or perform on your telephone from 5 p.m. to 11 p.m. every night. You would be appalled. This is exactly the demand made by 'the machine' on the companies that run it. Made, like telephone, morse code, smoke signals, fog horns, Very lights, to send messages in moments of need, television finds itself required to transmit continuously, regardless of need. And there the problem lies.

How does television create a need for itself?

Nobody *needs* hour after hour of television in the way that a sick man needs a doctor or a crying child needs its mother. Yet, to justify their existence and pay their way, the television companies have to make themselves needed. And this they can only do by encouraging the *habit* of viewing; the theory is that once a viewing habit has been formed, a need has been created.

How is the habit created?

A glance at the *Radio Times* or *TV Times* reveals a pattern of programmes repeated week after week at exactly the same time. The effect is to make the viewer associate a particular programme with a particular time on a particular evening. Though it is not a part of his job, his house or his family, the regular appearance of a television programme can *seem* an essential part of a man's life. But to create and then fill this need in the viewing population a programme must not vary by much its time, or its main characters, or its tone or its format. Do a survey yourself. When you hear someone say they have to get home to see television, note how often it is because the programme is an old favourite; how often because a programme is new.

Is there a need?

The answer is clearly yes. Extensive viewing habits are a form of addiction. And chronic smokers will tell you that there is nothing imaginary about their need for a cigarette. A need it may be, but is it a worthy need? That is harder to answer.

Four scripts

Z Cars

by Keith Dewhurst
Ronald Eyre
John Hopkins
and Alan Plater

by arrangement with the British Broadcasting Corporation

selected for reading in Secondary Schools
and edited by

Michael Marland B A

Headmaster, Woodberry Down School

with an introduction by
Ronald Eyre

Longman

LONGMAN GROUP LIMITED
London

*Associated companies, branches and representatives
throughout the world*

This edition © Longman Group Ltd (formerly
Longmans, Green & Co Ltd) 1968

First published 1968
New impression 1974

ISBN 0 582 23371 2

*Printed in Hong Kong by
Peninsula Press Ltd*

People feel that they need only what they already know. So the need-makers of television tend to distrust the unfamiliar, and encourage a mixture of repetition only topped off with novelty. The effect is to present an audience with what look like new delights but never to make the newness so disturbing that a man switches off his set in order to sit down and think. This policy, if analysed, implies disrespect for the viewers. It supposes that most viewers are not open to new experiences, do not enjoy exploring the world around them and are not adventurous. This may be so, but all the best teaching, preaching, and writing is based on the hope that this is not always so.

Are the programme producing companies the villains?

The wiser television bodies know this situation and they are constantly (though less and less) spending money on programmes that break new ground, and may as a result have only a small audience. But the main draw in the TV output (apart from the odd events of national importance) is the drama series. This, with all the pressures from programme planners, from 'responsible outside bodies', from viewers, from the critics, and with its inbuilt tendency to staleness and repetition, is the slot into which *Z Cars* fitted.

What does a 'Z Cars' writer start with?

The original *Z Cars* writer, Troy Kennedy Martin, started with nothing except a desire to tell stories about police life as, after research, he knew it to be. The writers who followed inherited the series framework: a location, a set of characters and an attitude to the material. Of these the last mattered most.

An attitude

From the start *Z Cars* concentrated on the work of the police rather than on the exploits of criminals. And where the criminal and the law met, the interest was invariably on how the police dealt with a variety of situations. If the series had been a series of dramatised crimes, the effect would have been to make the criminal (until he was caught) the hero, and leave to the police the repetitive and servile work of pursuit and capture. But *Z Cars* always looked not merely at the criminal but at the community through police eyes. In this way it showed what it is like to be a policeman and it lit up some of the complexities of law and order in a modern, urban society.

The policeman is often over-worked, tired, with limited patience, limited sympathy, and limited knowledge. He is picked out and isolated in a special uniform, confronted by every variety of disturbance, misfortune, extremity of behaviour. He is employed by society as a guardian and watch dog. The old figure of a cheery, size-twelve, slow-moving paternal 'bobby' was appropriate to a village society where everybody knew everybody else and there were a limited number of possible suspects for any crime. The modern city is very different; a place where rootless people take rooms, eye one another, and keep themselves to themselves; where the old can die of cold unnoticed; where a vast acreage of offices and shops are deserted every night at 5.30; where a cry in the street may mean a dying man, a drunken man, an angry man, or just a man having a joke.

In these circumstances a new attitude to the law and the police is needed, an attitude tuned in to the realities of this century. And this attitude could be seen in the best of *Z Cars*.

'Z Cars' and police reaction

The earlier *Z Cars* stories met with police opposition, although the material was drawn from police sources. Behind the opposition was a feeling that public respect for the police would decline if its members were shown as sometimes making mistakes, turbulent, ambitious, complacent: in fact, human. But by the time it ended *Z Cars* had universal police support. What happened to make the change? Two things.

First, the police were reassured, as the series went on, that for a policeman to show human weakness did not diminish public respect for the uniform. It might even inspire public sympathy. (Incidentally, were they right?) Secondly, the series without a doubt changed its nature and towards the end there were fewer scripts that offered any sort of comment on law and society and more that told a simple tale of crime and detection. The series became safe as it became stale.

What is worth recalling of 'Z Cars'?

Now and again from start to finish of the series a writer took these stock characters—Barlow, Watt, the lads, the crooks— as he might take the stock characters of a legend and used them to say important things: The attitude to law is changing; the city is creating new stresses; the British Empire has died; Britannia doesn't rule the waves; class is losing its old caste marks and finding new ones.

In some of the episodes, the writer explored disturbing questions: Who is more criminal, the housebreaker or the slum landlord? Who makes the criminal what he is? Is he entirely responsible himself? When a law is unjust, is it criminal to break it? Can we care for people we do not know? Can we know anybody by looking at his face or watching his actions? Can we judge him even when we think we know him? What is the right thing to do? Who cares?

These are *our* situations. These are *our* questions. To ask them is not disrespectful, insolent, or morbid. It is a sign of life. The scripts that follow ask these questions too, not in so many words, but in their own dramatic terms: Barlow confronting colour prejudice; running Milligan trapped and telling fairy tales; Lynch making heavy weather of a pair of lost gloves while a man he has just left gases himself; Watt ordered to take an action which he knows to be both inevitable and wrong—none of these men knows the answers. The scripts themselves do not give easy answers either; their value to us is that they raise the questions.

A Quiet Night

'It's been a quiet night,' says Inspector Barlow in the very first *Z Cars* of all (*Four Of A Kind*, by Troy Kennedy Martin) after his men have dealt with a fight in a pub, a madman running berserk with an axe, two girls on the run from home and into danger, and a gang of thieves stealing a lorry. And he was not being sarcastic. Every night is critical for somebody. Go to bed early and sleep and, for all you know, everyone else is asleep as well. Get up in the middle of the night, and you'll find the odd bedroom light on, someone walking up the street, a car passing, someone shouting: all the signs that for somebody or other it is a night of crisis—if not for you.

Alan Plater's script presents one such night in Newtown.

What happens?

☐ For Nicholson it is a crisis night—he has quarrelled with his wife and he has left home.

☐ For Regan it is *the* crisis night—he gases himself.

☐ It is crisis night, too, for characters who are mentioned but do not appear.

☐ Bob Stewart, the housebreaker, is caught climbing through a lavatory window.

☐ Councillor Purvis sees a man dribbling a ball of fish-and-chip paper up the road, and feels disturbed enough to ring the police.

☐ The night is as tense and busy as any other night but for the men at Newtown it is uneventful.

How do the police react?

In moments of crisis and action these policemen are (on the evidence of other *Z Cars* stories) still, relaxed, poised, observant. Tonight they are bored. 'Restless, John?', says

Blackitt. And Watt answers, 'Everything's so flaming peaceful.' Underemployment makes unexpected demands on these men and it is worth seeing how they are met.

Watt, for one, becomes agitated and his way out is to exchange reminiscences with Blackitt, as if the only alternative to action in the present is the recollection of action in the past. When they are not reminiscing they tell jokes. So do the patrolmen. But the police constables joke about the Chief Inspector, whereas the sergeants joke about a slightly wider range of subjects.

Why do men in particular circumstances tell jokes? Do they tell sensible jokes? What are the circumstances in which they tell them? Do jokes make living together easier?

The uses of inactivity

Men in a critical situation usually have a sense of priorities. Men at ease lose it. On a busy night Lynch would have no time to fret about his lost gloves and Fancy Smith would not feel such elaborate guilt about bumping a car and not owning up. After all, compared with robbery, murder, arson, these are small things. But during 'a quiet night' there is time for them. And the value of revealing these small worries to the audience is that they show up the real Lynch, the real Graham, and the real Smith. On a busy night the patrolmen may see more action but, from an audience's point of view, the differences between the men would tend to be ironed out.

Regan and Lynch

Regan is a drunk in a pub talking about darts. Because he is known by both the publican and Lynch, he is taken home and put to bed. For once a Newtown policeman can behave like a village bobby because he knows the man. The attitude of the other attendant policeman is more usual. Detective Constable Elliott assumes that Regan will be charged. Graham resents the amount of time that Lynch is spending on a single case of drunkenness. But Regan is a person not just 'a case' and his story emerges gradually.

7

In his day he was a notable darts player who took on and defeated all comers. His skill gave him a status among his friends; it reassured and toughened him. Then an accident at work ruined his darts hand and he became no more than an onlooker. Bitterness, isolation and despair followed. The knowledge of this affected and softened the behaviour of those who knew him. So that Lynch can say, against all the evidence. 'He's not drunk . . . just a bit off colour'—a piece of friendliness that Regan remembers when he reaches his squalid room. He offers a cup of tea that Lynch refuses, pleading other things to do. And Regan slips from the story, until near the end Mrs Fletcher, whose sense of smell has provoked police action before, reports a gas leak. And Regan is found dead.

At this moment the self-recrimination starts. Why did Lynch not accept the cup of tea? It might have helped Regan past the crisis, at least for that night. How could Lynch say that what he had to do could matter more than drinking that particular cup of tea? But how was he to know that a cup of tea could matter all that much? Lynch believes he let a man down—fatally. Did he?

Nicholson

The audience have expectations as they watch *Z Cars*. And the sight of a man drifting round the streets alone, lighting cigarettes, sitting on benches, especially when he is glimpsed from time to time in the story without explanation, is enough to label him 'crook'. When the police are on the look-out for a housebreaker of roughly similar age and appearance it is enough to put him under suspicion, to audience and police alike. It is Alan Plater's great skill that he leads the police and the audience into making a judgment on Nicholson. Then he clarifies the man and his plight and throws suspicion back from Nicholson to the police and the audience who have dared to jump to and act on wrong conclusions.

Nicholson is locked out after a row with his wife. He will go back after his taste of 'freedom', which he isn't really enjoying. 'Why don't you go home?' Lynch asks.

Nicholson: 'Stupid. Don't laugh, will you? It's just I thought I might . . . like it, not going home, thought I might like it.'

Lynch: 'You mean freedom?'

Nicholson: 'I thought I might, but it's stupid, at my age . . . you only look a fool. And you feel the cold as well, and I didn't know what to do . . . where to go, and I said to her, I'm not coming back and I thought I might like it. Don't laugh.'

Nicholson sums up a common impulse and a common reaction. What he's feeling out in the cold is felt by children who run away in a bad temper, and turn back when night draws in and the streets become unfamiliar; by quixotic Englishmen who emigrate and find the same problems facing them in Australia as they shunned in England; by most people after a row where the ties of need and affection with a person, a home or a country are stronger than the momentary impulse to break them. Nicholson's quiet night on the streets may alter his whole life.

A quiet night?

The police would say that 'a quiet night' is a fair description. By that they mean that they have copped no burglars, discovered no corpses, tracked no suspects, blown no whistles, made no entries in their notebooks. But the audience is left knowing that, like all nights, it is a night of crisis—for somebody, and that our reactions to people when we first see them may lack real understanding.

Window Dressing

Terry Greenhalgh feels the need to demonstrate. His first demonstration is trivial. He rearranges the goods in a shop. He neither steals nor destroys. Order could be restored in an hour. His second demonstration is more serious involving damage to property. In both cases what he does is a form of 'window dressing' for his own feelings. The importance of his acts is not in themselves but in his condition which they conceal. Greenhalgh is in difficulties.

His surroundings

His mother and his employer have one thing in common. They are scared. His mother, brought up in the strong Puritan tradition of right behaviour and godliness, sees in everything her son does a deviation from the right path. His conversation, interests, friends and the contents of his pockets are unfamiliar—therefore evil. Her fear clouds her vision, limits her sympathies, shrinks her understanding. She carries an air of doom around with her. The sight of the police on her doorstep does not surprise her. She expects it; just as surely as she expects judgement for sinners and 'rewards' for the righteous in the after-life, to which she doggedly looks forward. In the meantime her husband sits coughing and complaining in the kitchen.

For Terry, with his sensitivity, this household is both terrifying and funny. He exaggerates and besmuts his stories just to find out how far he can lead his mother on. And, to his distress, he finds that her gullibility is limitless, she will believe anything.

Mercer too goes in terror. He sees around him signs and portents. 'They' (whoever 'they' are) are about to take over. Society is threatened. Action by vigilant people is needed. His fears, like Mrs Greenhalgh's, are ill-based, but once they are established evidence easily turns up to confirm them.

Thus Terry's probation record plus his unexpected temperament and manner are enough to turn Mercer into a witch-hunter. The background against which Terry moves both at home and at work is withdrawn and hysterical. His only hope is to find a new setting and, if not that, a new attitude to his old setting. But to do this he needs help.

The Probation Officer

Mr Mercer and Mrs Greenhalgh live in a nightmare world. Aspin, the Probation Officer, finds it more humdrum and more hopeful. Confronted by Greenhalgh, who thinks everyone is against him, Aspin adjusts the balance—'Once you're through this bad patch, you'll find it's about fifty-fifty. Half for you. Half against. A working proposition anyway.' He does not offer the boy any great hopes. But he does offer a fighting chance. And, being a lad of spirit, that is all that Greenhalgh needs. At this point the police cross his path.

Barlow and Watt

The key encounter in this story is not that of Aspin and Greenhalgh in the baths, nor Greenhalgh on the run and the police, nor anything in the disordered store at the beginning. These are all the extremities of the story. The key encounter is that of Watt and Barlow in the second half. Watt has called in the Probation Officer to help with the case, and Aspin presents a picture of Greenhalgh's character and background that quite contradicts what he has heard from other sources. Greenhalgh comes into perspective, and on Aspin's advice Watt strikes a bargain. The police are to delay picking Greenhalgh up in order to give him a chance to surrender voluntarily.

This involves a vital principle that Aspin summarises in conversation with Greenhalgh. 'If they catch you, they'll catch you like an animal. If you go to them, you'll walk like a man, eh?' All coercion, from manhandling to a firm hand on the collar, is an affront to a man's pride. It degrades him. And Aspin knows that the hope for Greenhalgh is to make him responsible for himself and proud of it. So that punishment (which is bound to come) is less an imposition from outside than an admission by the boy himself that he has broken the law and must pay for it.

For Watt this is not so much a new thought as one which police background and training do not encourage. But he has ventured from Newtown Police Station into the Probation Office and takes the consequences. He agrees to give Greenhalgh a chance, adding, ominously:

'You see it would be different if I were a free agent. But I'm not. I work for a boss.'

Indeed he does and his boss, Barlow, is in a very delicate position. The press, as they are apt to, have turned on the police and described them as 'inadequate and overworked'. On the phone regularly is Mr Mercer demanding action, speaking for all 'right-minded' members of the public. To justify himself as guardian of public safety Barlow wants immediate results. At this point Watt and Barlow, under their different pressures, meet.

Barlow takes a strict line.

'Lawbreaking is lawbreaking. It's not affected by background. If the magistrates want it to be that's their concern. But not yours.'

Too many crooks have tried to lead him a dance, and he prides himself on seeing through them. (Hasn't he just refused to take in old Carroll, who wanted the safety and regular meal times of a prison cell?) Barlow in this script, like Lowther in *A Place Of Safety*, cannot afford to be soft. He is not brutal. He understands Watt's concern. He may even share it. But, as a man committed to making the police system work, he cannot act on it. When Watt recklessly calls ordinary police work 'a job for barbarians', Barlow has his reply:

'Then you're a sergeant barbarian, Watt. That's not bad. And I'm an inspector barbarian. That's even better. Folk must take us as they find us.'

These are the words of either a thug and a gauleiter, or of an intelligent man who is putting a delicate situation crudely.

Barlow being Barlow, it is likely to be the latter, but to Aspin, standing on the swimming-bath steps and watching Greenhalgh dragged away, things must seem very different.

Hope for Greenhalgh

Aspin guides Greenhalgh to a decision that no other sort of pressure could produce. The boy volunteers to give himself up. In other words, he trusts Aspin and on Aspin's recommendation he is ready to trust the police. The presence of Graham and Baker outside the baths undoes everything that Aspin has done and yet another 'animal' is dragged struggling into Newtown Police Station. Greenhalgh is betrayed, Aspin is betrayed, Watt is betrayed; Mercer is accommodated; Mrs Greenhalgh justified; the law has taken its course but at what cost?

Greenhalgh has one lifeline, the trust he has built up with Aspin. Can it ever be restored? How will Watt feel when next he needs to consult the Probation Service? Will the removal of Greenhalgh convince Mercer that he is safe? What good can come out of a mess like this?

On the other hand, consider Barlow's position. If society is to be guarded, mustn't there always be some innocent casualties? And isn't the real question not so much 'Why must there be innocent casualties?' as 'How do we keep their numbers down?'

An extension

Barlow and Aspin stand at opposite poles in this story. Yet they never meet. Surely the hottest scene of all is missing. Imagine that Aspin asks to see Barlow and, for the first time, the two men face one another under the shadow of the events of the play. How do you think that scene would go?

Running Milligan

The bare bones

Milligan is serving a sentence for robbery with violence. He has one month to go before release. His wife Margaret dies and he is let out on parole to attend the funeral. He fails to honour his parole and the police have to find, collect and return him.

This is a piece of routine police work. Given that robbery with violence is a serious crime, given that imprisonment is the appropriate punishment for it and given that a wife's funeral provides grounds compassionate enough for a convict to be paroled, the job of the police should be straightforward. They have to make sure that Milligan returns and completes his sentence. No more.

But the story of running Milligan raises wider questions than that. He is a weak man. Can he help that? His upbringing has been unfortunate. Is he to blame? His relatives and acquaintances (for they are not real friends) do not offer help. Can you blame them? It is to Inspector Barlow's credit that, though he still does what he has to do, he understands more than anybody else the difficulties of Milligan's position.

Alderman Wilson

It seems odd to mention such a small character so early, but Wilson's importance is that he speaks with all the confidence and finality of a really ignorant man: 'This man you're looking for; you know, the convict .... Pretty low type I suppose, is he? Eh?'

'Well, you know, sir', hedges Blackitt.

'I do. I know 'em inside out.' It is this bumptiousness that the Milligan story challenges.

Milligan

Milligan is a problem man (in some ways a problem child). He combines violence with whimpering, both signs of his inner lostness. He has never grown up; but instead of Peter Pan's never-never land he has the here-and-now of Newtown and Seaport, and this he cannot face. Hence the running.

Parole

Milligan is released for a few hours to attend his wife's funeral. The parole is 'compassionate'. Certainly the man who allow it are feeling compassion, but are they doing the best they can for Milligan? Barlow raises the point:

'Parole itself—well meant but ridiculuous.' Blackitt does not really agree. Barlow insists:

'Come on. You know it is.' He doesn't explain himself till later.

'I've told you. It's common. A man comes out on parole and if he thinks it's going to be a little bit of freedom he's wrong. It isn't. Leaving prison's painful. It's like leaving your bed for the first time when you've had a leg amputated. But that's not all he has to face. Oh no. They've let him out for a heart-breaking like his wife's funeral.'

Milligan's parole, meant to be compassionate, becomes an act of cruelty. With only a month more to serve he is released, in a state of high emotion, into a situation he cannot stand up to. The result for Milligan is an extended sentence. Is 'compassion' enough?

The sister-in-law's

Milligan's children are staying with his dead wife's sister-in-law, Cath and her husband, Jack. And Milligan comes to their house for the first time on this parole. Immediately, apart from the distress of the funeral, he walks into a situation of high tension. For a start Jack and Cath have been rehoused; their neighbours are new people. With their new life in Newtown they want to forget their old life in Seaport, but Milligan's presence reminds them of it. Secondly, Cath wants Milligan to remove his children as soon as he is released and she tells him so. The reason is not lack of money or space. (Barlow offers to try and help her.) She simply rejects him:

Cath: I—I told him that when he comes out of prison, see, when he—he can take his kids and get out. Out. All of 'em.

Barlow: I see.

Cath: Do you?

Barlow: Yes. Every day of the week.

Cath: All right.

Cath's last two words are important. She will never be persuaded. Her rejection of Milligan is complete. She cannot be even shamed into helping him.

Cathy and Milligan

Cath feels bound to tolerate her husband and her father, though one is weak and evasive and the other malicious. And there was a time when she tolerated Milligan too. More than that. She 'fancied' him. But now she sees him as he is; a combination of the worst traits of husband and father, and having no obligations to him she rejects him. Decisively.

Is she a victim or a villain?

Who is to blame if Milligan's children are neglected or take to crime?

What is the future for Sandra?

Which brings us to Milly.

Milly

Milly, the Seaport prostitute, does the one act of kindness in the whole story. She gives Milligan money and to save his pride she turns away while he takes it. This is the thanks she gets:

Milligan: (talking about his wife) She—er—she was a very pure girl, you know.

Milly: Was she?

Milligan: She wasn't like you.

Milly: Thank you.

Milligan: I mean; she didn't have the understanding.

But she knows that he said what he meant the first time. 'I'll bet you were sorry when your mother died, weren't you?' says Milly, touching the heart of the matter.

Ganger and Harry

These two, in the eyes of the law, are less blameworthy than Milly. They did *not* help an escaped convict; unless Ganger's prayer and Harry's advice to keep running could be called 'help'. The scene with these two illustrates how speech can be a way of preventing communication. Both of them are ready with friendly advice, and no doubt the tone of their voices is urgent and warm. But their intention is to lose Milligan as soon as they safely can and he, being a sensitive man, sees beyond the comradely chat, the blank wall of their rejection. On Harry's advice, he makes for the old railway station where he comes face-to-face with Whisky. Also on Harry's advice, the police follow and catch him.

Whisky

The high-point of Keith Dewhurst's script, and the episode which cannot be paraphrased, but has to be accepted and relished on its own dramatic terms, is the confrontation of Whisky and Milligan. It takes place in a room all the more stale and isolated because outside it are railway lines, trains, bridges, signals, all the signs of movement, communication, purpose, activity. For Milligan it is indeed the end of the line. In that room he catches his own reflection as it might be in a waiting-room mirror. But instead of a literal re-production of his own features, Milligan sees a portrait of himself gone-to-bits. And that portrait is Whisky.

Whisky and Milligan are split images of the same man. Whisky hopes to escape life by drinking; Milligan by running. Whisky is shell-shocked; Milligan, life-shocked. Whisky, in his weakness, has survived, leaving stronger men straddled on the barbed wire; Milligan, in *his* weakness, has survived, leaving his wife to struggle and die keeping the family going. Whisky wants to hear a story. Milligan likes stories too and the best of them have him as a hero. Both Whisky and Milligan have the body of a man and the nature of a child, and in this maimed condition they are asked to face adult life.

Summary

The story of Milligan sets against the needs of law and order and public safety the fact of a man who breaks the law through his own weakness.

To what extent can we afford to be sympathetic?

This man Milligan attacked another man and robbed him. But who is Milligan? Can he be separated from the society that made him? We do not punish a one-legged man because he cannot run. Have we any more right to punish a man with a weak character because he cannot keep himself in order? What rights have the people he may attack next? Can we be 'fair' with a case like this? Is there such a thing as justice?

A place of safety

Take a man. A warrant is out for his arrest. He hides. When the warrant officer persists, the man stabs him. What should the police do? The answer is obvious.

Now look at the situation again. A man with a dark skin, living in a squalid tenement, unused to the ways of a European city, unable to do the job he was trained for, with a wife who falls for the blandishments of hire-purchase firms, gets himself into debt. The firms sue him. The officer who delivers the warrant is a thug. He harries his prey. The prey turns on him and, as a way (he thinks) of protecting his room, his wife and his children, he attacks. The warrant officer is wounded. What should the police do now?

Let the thug look after himself? Protect the immigrant? If so, what about all the other cases in which ignorance and thoughtlessness lead to debt and debt leads to violence? John Hopkins's script collars the audience and makes them face the complications of the case so that at the end, like Barlow and Fancy Smith, we are relieved to turn our attention to something straightforward—like housebreaking, riot, theft. If, indeed, anything is ever straightforward.

Sadik and Nana

The immigrant and his wife have about them a touch of nobility. The stabbing which starts the story shocks the stabber as much as the stabbed. It shows him a side of his nature that he did not know.

'I am most frightened of myself. I find this anger in me—hatred. Deep in me—and I am afraid of it. The man hunted me—shouted at me—cursed me—like an animal—and I turned like an animal.'

Sadik has modesty and clear-sightedness. He is articulate about his plight. In a sense he believes he deserves it and sees in the loss of his freedom, his family, his room and his job a just punishment. It is up to us, standing aloof, to agree or disagree. After all, when in *Macbeth* we see the murderers trap Lady Macduff we wish she had Sadik's knife and his strong arm to help her. Even the 'diminutive wren' is allowed to defend her nest. May not Sadik do the same?

Sadik has an open mind. His wife's has closed. She comes from more varied stock. She knows more of the world. Her expectations are fewer. To her, a warrant officer beating at the door, interfering drunks at the bus stop, Jock, Fancy and Watt trying to get her a place to sleep are just different facets of the same thing: brutal, playful, embarrassed, guilt-ridden English colour prejudice. Hers is the voice of true disillusion:

Nana: 'You were expecting me to say thank you?' *Fancy*: 'I said nothing.' *Nana*: 'Why should I thank you? What have you done? . . . You've done no more than your duty—as a policeman. Had you been men—men like those men—jeering at me—ordinary men—would you have done as much?' That bitterness is not the product of one day's work; it is the legacy of centuries. What can be done to sweeten it? How long will it take? Have we all that time to spare?

The tenement house

This building, which dominates the start of the story, is a physical expression of the lives the inmates lead. It is a ghetto. Each room is a cell. The landlord is an absentee. Mrs Lunt squats at the bottom of the stairs as caretaker and watchdog. It is dangerous to approach neighbours. It is better to be deaf to shouts and scurryings outside your own four walls. If a man is lying bleeding on the stairs, step over him and carry on. If the police are called, say nothing. If you must be inquisitive, stand inside your own room and look through a crack in the door. If someone approaches your door, shut it. If they knock, bolt it. Village life, tribal life, all healthy society, involves connections and hierarchies and neighbourliness and gossip and interference and mutual help and common endeavour. Life in the tenement has none of these. Families are juxtaposed but not linked. There is no social life. The crumbling walls, the filthy staircase are the outward signs of this inward disease. And in some sense, though perhaps less extremely, the 'tenement rot' affects all our gigantic ailing cities.

Mrs Lunt

This woman, left behind in the tenement as the natives moved out and the immigrants moved in, is only important because of the thousands she speaks for. Her mind is as closed as Nana's, the only distinction being that she had less to open in the first place. Her picture of a 'blackie' is built up from gossip, sensational press reports, and a squinting scrutiny of the inmates moving up and down the stairs. 'I read where one of them blackies did his own family in,' she says, and thinks that what one did all might do. She could just as truthfully have said: 'I read where one of them blackies won the Noble prize.'

It comes as a relief to find that Mrs Lunt's ignorance and malice are not confined to the immigrants. She has similar fantasies about the police. When Mr Isaacs, a charitable man trapped in an uncharitable house, volunteers to talk to the police, she warns him: 'Likely lock you away. Set foot in there. That's what they'll do. You go speaking up for blackies—likely lock you away.'

Mrs Lunt by herself is funny. Multiplied, as she is in fact, into thousands upon thousands, she is a monster.

Police attitudes

In terms of pursuit and capture, the police clean up the Sadik case quite neatly. Sadik is imprisoned. His wife and family are variously housed. Wallace has got his own back. But in human terms, they have cleaned up nothing. All they have done is split open a social sore and we are left gazing at it. All the officers are affected. Weir and Watt clash over the rehousing of Nana and the children. Fancy Smith is infuriated at the scuttling indifference of the tenement on-lookers. Only Barlow understands, feels for, and finally despairs of the vast difficulties of the Sadik case.

Barlow

As a practising policeman, Barlow can twist the truth to suit himself. He lies to Sadik and his excuse would be the need to disarm a dangerous man. His coolness and dishonesty in this instance shock the bystanders—both audience and police. But on the wider issue of Sadik's guilt and the right way to treat him, Barlow is sensitive and humane. And his position is stated and explored in the confrontation with Inspector Lowther of the Warrant Department. Lowther's position is simple.

'There's only one way to keep them under.... If you show you're soft—show weakness—d'you think they'll respect you? They'll laugh in your face.'

And he accuses Barlow of making a special case of this. In his own more articulate way, Lowther is on the side of Mrs Lunt.

Barlow, by contrast, makes distinctions.

'It is a special case! Isn't it? Here's a man—he's never hurt anyone the whole of his life ... suddenly one bright summer evening he clobbers a bloke with a hatchet. Come on, isn't that special?' How would you reply? And if your answer is 'yes' another question follows: 'How is this case more special than other cases?' And if your answer to that is that it is special but not *more* special, yet another question follows: 'How are the codifications of law, judgment, punishment, the assignment of blame to be settled if no two cases are ever alike?'

Barlow and Lowther are both roused but in different ways. Lowther has no doubts about the right course of action. His only fears are that the police will be soft on a near-killer. Barlow, confessing to his own form of colour prejudice, having no doubts about his role as a policeman, complacent about the occasional lie and the occasional need for violence, cannot satisfy himself that in the case of Sadik justice has been done. If it were only Sadik, of course he, might in time forget. But he sees the issues beyond the Sadik case—immigration, city life, separation into cells, poverty, fear, publicity and persuasion, wealth ... and he has no answer.

No wonder he turns hopefully to the Station map and is relieved when the phone rings to report something more easily dealt with. He looks for relief. But, even if it comes, we know the relief will only be temporary.

The Personnel of Victor Division

C.I.D.

Detective Chief Inspector Barlow

Detective Sergeant Watt

Uniform Branch

Sergeant Blackitt

PC Sweet

PC Taylor (*on telephone*)

PC John Elliot (*off duty*)

Crime Patrol

Z Victor One
PC Jock Weir

PC Fancy Smith

Z Victor Two
PC Herbert Lynch

PC Baker

PC David Graham

A Quiet Night by Alan Plater

The Cast

Detective Sergeant John Watt
Sergeant Blackitt
PC Jock Weir
PC Fancy Smith
PC David Graham
PC Herbert Lynch
PC Ian Sweet
Detective Constable John Elliot
Shirley Burscough, on duty in the Information Room
Mr Preston, landlord of *The Flying Horse* public house
Mrs Preston
Mr Nicholson, a neatly dressed man in his late forties
Jimmy Oliver, owner of a garage
Tim Regan, a shabbily dressed man in his late fifties
Mrs French, an elderly lady who lodges in the same house
Mr Simpson, an ex-military man who also lodges in the
    same house
Dr Nelson
PC Haywood
Freda, who serves in the Police canteen
Ambulance men

A Quiet Night

The police canteen one night

(*The atmosphere is relaxed and cheerful, and it is fairly noisy. A number of constables are sitting drinking tea, including Jock. Fancy and Graham who are listening to Sweet telling a funny story.*)

SWEET In his birthday suit . . .

FANCY Oh aye . . .

(*Lynch enters.*)

LYNCH Dave?

SWEET Stark naked he was . . .

(*Lynch crossing to the table*)

LYNCH Are you ready, Dave?—Stark naked? Who was?

SWEET Mr Barlow . . .

GRAHAM Hang on, Bert . . .

JOCK Ian's telling us a funny story . . .

LYNCH Disgusting.

SWEET Anyhow, there he is, nowt on, only his helmet . . .

(*Lynch makes a face.*)

FANCY Getaway!

SWEET And up comes Mr Robins and he says, 'Charlie, what you doing waving your arms about?' . . . and Mr Barlow says 'I'm directing the traffic' so Robins says, 'Why haven't you got any clothes on Charlie?' . . . so Mr Barlow says, 'Well it's the middle of the night there isn't much traffic . . . so . . .

LYNCH Mr Robins says . . .

SWEET (*simultaneously*) Mr Robins says . . . 'What you got your helmet on for?'

FANCY (*laughing*) What you got your helmet on for?

JOCK I don't believe it.

SWEET So Mr Barlow says, 'Well, there might be an odd car . . .'

(*Jock and Fancy laugh. Lynch curls a lip in contempt. Graham does not react.*)

GRAHAM (*flatly*) Yes. Good joke that. Very good.

LYNCH (*impatiently*) Are you coming?

GRAHAM Aye. (*He stands up, picks up his cap and moves to door with Lynch.*) Some of us have got work to do.

JOCK Now just watch it!

(*Jock gets up in mock-threatening pose but Lynch and Graham exit quickly. Jock sits down again, smiling.*)

FANCY Cheeky devils!

JOCK Rather them than me.

FANCY On nights.

SWEET Get bored stiff, nowt to do . . . just at the moment, like . . .

FANCY Hey, Ian, what was that about Mr Barlow?

SWEET Eh?

FANCY (*dead pan*) Without his clothes on, you were saying . . .?

The Station office

(*Watt has just come in, and is in his raincoat and hat. Blackitt is behind the counter.*)

WATT Can't understand it, Tommy Forrest . . .

BLACKITT Funny, that.

WATT There in the bar—saw me—'Evening' he says.

BLACKITT Likely didn't recognise you.

WATT Must be four, five years since he spoke to me . . .

BLACKITT Been away for three of them has Tommy . . .

WATT (*thoughtfully*) Aye.

(*Watt has taken off his hat and coat and goes into C.I.D. room to hang them up as Lynch and Graham enter.*)

BLACKITT Raring to be off then, lads?

GRAHAM Can't hardly wait.

LYNCH It's a man's life in the force.

BLACKITT If you don't weaken.

(*Lynch and Graham exit.*)

Back in the canteen

(*We see Fancy, Jock and Sweet, talking together*)

JOCK I just don't feel like it, that's all . . .

SWEET He's signed the pledge.

FANCY (*standing up*) Well I'm going for a pint, you can please yourself . . .

JOCK Aye, O.K.

FANCY (*to Sweet*) He's getting old, that's what it is . . .

JOCK Pack it in, Fancy . . .

FANCY (*breaking in*) Oh hell, Jock!

JOCK What's wrong?

FANCY Bert Lynch, and Dave . . . we forgot to tell them . . .

JOCK It's your fault, you were supposed to remember . . .

FANCY Aye, I know but . . .

JOCK You did it . . .

FANCY I might just catch them, see you, lads . . .

(*Fancy exits in a great hurry.*)

SWEET What's up, Jock?

JOCK Nothing. Just . . . nothing . . .

The C.I.D. room

(*Watt is sitting on his desk browsing through crime reports. He puts them down, and crosses to the door.*)

The Station office

(*Watt enters. Blackitt looks up.*)

BLACKITT Looking for something, John?

WATT I don't know.

(*Watt starts turning over papers behind the desk, obviously looking for something. Fancy enters.*)

FANCY Hey, Sarge have the lads gone?

BLACKITT What, Bert Lynch and Dave?

FANCY Aye.

BLACKITT Just this minute gone out . . .

FANCY Blast!

BLACKITT Can I give them a message . . . when they come in?

FANCY Er . . . no . . . no, I don't think so. (*pause*) Good night.
(*Fancy exits.*)

BLACKITT (*puzzled*) Night. (*Watt is still searching.*) Restless, John?

WATT Everything's so flaming peaceful . . .

BLACKITT You know why.

WATT Mind you, I did hear . . . yes, I know why it is . . .

Interior of Z Victor Two

(*Lynch is driving.*)

GRAHAM I'll tell you why it is.

LYNCH Freddie Bishop and his mates getting knocked off . . .

GRAHAM Thirty seven other offences, thirty seven . . .

LYNCH Makes me laugh, Dave, seeing a layabout like Freddie in court, all dressed up, white shirt, Sunday suit. Old mum saying 'He always helps me with the washing up' . . . washing up! Only goes home about once a month.

GRAHAM You heard the solicitor bloke . . . Freddie's not a bad lad, he's just misguided.

LYNCH Misguided my . . . foot!

GRAHAM Anyhow, it's keeping them quiet . . . for a bit.

LYNCH Temporary, Dave.

GRAHAM They're all right. (*Laconically*) Just a bit misguided.

The Station office

(*Watt and Blackitt are still talking.*)

WATT Aye, Bob Stewart, you remember him?

BLACKITT Should do, I've knocked him off twice. Years ago I'm talking about now . . .

(*Jock enters from the canteen.*)

BLACKITT Night, Jock . . .

WATT Night, lad . . .

JOCK Night . . .

WATT Well, I'm stood again the bar and I hear this bloke saying something about Bob Stewart, said he's seen him . . .

(*Watt realises that Jock has returned to the counter and is waiting to speak to Blackitt.*)

BLACKITT Well?

JOCK Sorry to bust in, but . . . did you see Fancy Smith when he went out?

BLACKITT Aye, about five minutes ago . . .

JOCK He was looking for Bert Lynch, wasn't he?

BLACKITT That's right.

JOCK Did he find him?

BLACKITT No. Why?

JOCK Nothing . . . doesn't matter . . .

WATT (*who has been listening with puzzled interest*) What's going on?

BLACKITT Don't ask me . . .

JOCK Nothing very important . . .

BLACKITT (*as Jock exits*) It's crime cars, they've formed a secret society, Ku Klux Klan; that's what's happening . . .

WATT (*to Jock as he exits*) Sleep it off, lad.

BLACKITT Gets you that way after a bit . . . when it's quiet.

WATT Aye.

(*There is a pause.*)

BLACKITT You were stood at the bar . . .

WATT And I heard somebody mention Bob Stewart . . .

BLACKITT Well as far as I know, Bobby moved to Birmingham . . . did a few jobs there, got done again . . .

WATT Aye, I thought so . . .

BLACKITT Did you know him, this feller doing the talking?

WATT Never seen him before but he was with Tommy Forrest . . .

BLACKITT All sticking together . . .

WATT Funny, isn't it?

BLACKITT What?

WATT   Always grumbling about having too much to do and soon as things get quiet . . . you start looking for excuses to start something . . .

BLACKITT   (*doubtfully*) Maybe . . .

WATT   Eh?

BLACKITT   Well, it's maybe only a casual remark in a pub, like; all the same I'd check with records . . . see if there's been any jobs that . . .

WATT   Any jobs Bob Stewart might have done?

BLACKITT   Aye.

WATT   I've checked.

BLACKITT   Is there any?

WATT   (*confidently*) Yes.

(*Watt goes into the C.I.D. office.*)

Inside Z Victor Two

(*Lynch is glancing out of the window.*)

LYNCH   Pubs are quiet.

GRAHAM   Everything's quiet.

LYNCH   It's not natural.

GRAHAM   I'm not complaining.

A street in Newtown

(*Cut to shot of Z Victor Two cruising down the street in the centre of Newtown. The camera pans with the patrol car, until we see a public house. The car continues, but the camera holds the pub, zooming in for a closer shot.*)

Inside the pub

(*We see a close shot of a dartboard as three darts land in quick succession.*)

PRESTON   (*heard off screen*) Last orders, please!

(*Cut to Mr and Mrs Preston landlord and wife—standing behind the bar. Mrs Preston is warm and cheerful; Mr Preston is quieter, perhaps a little tired.*)

MRS PRESTON   They're not rushing, love.

PRESTON   Makes a change.

MRS PRESTON   Been the same all night, dead quiet . . .

ELLIOT   Half of bitter please . . .

PRESTON   Half of bitter . . .

ELLIOT   Thanks.

PRESTON   (*to Mrs Preston*) It's quiet ones that bother me . . .

(*Preston looks towards Regan and Nicholson. Elliot turns to look. Cut to 2-shot of Regan and Nicholson. Nicholson is in his late forties, small, neatly dressed without being elegant—his appearance suggests an efficient clerk.*)

He sits on a stool, a shade ill at ease and nervous. Regan sits behind the table on a built-in seat. In his late fifties, he is dressed rather shabbily and looks very weary, rather than drunk. Even when he speaks, he tends to be withdrawn—as if talking to himself and not expecting any reply.

REGAN It's wrong, you know, all wrong.

NICHOLSON You what . . . I beg your pardon?

REGAN Double nineteen, double sixteen, that's his finish.

NICHOLSON Is it?

(Nicholson realises Regan is talking about the darts. We cut to x 2-shot of Elliot and Preston.)

PRESTON Not on duty tonight?

ELLIOT I'm always on duty.

PRESTON I suppose you are.

(Cut to 2-shot of Regan and Nicholson.)

REGAN Messing about with tops, can't see owt else but twenties, most of them.

NICHOLSON I'm a billiards man, myself.

REGAN There you are, see?

NICHOLSON Yes, I see what you mean.

(But we realise that he doesn't.)

REGAN *(scornfully)* Fifteen to split.

PRESTON *(heard off screen)* Last orders please!

NICHOLSON *(rising)* Well, I'll have to be off . . . off home.

REGAN Fifteen to split.

NICHOLSON Bit late as it is, like . . . good night . . . *(He goes out quickly.)*

REGAN Aye. *(He leans back in the corner and closes his eyes.)* Night . . .

(Cut to a close shot of Preston's reaction as he watches Tim Regan anxiously.)

Inside Z Victor Two

GRAHAM Nowt doing on trading estate, either.

LYNCH Got quiet up there when we had the light nights.

GRAHAM Never got started again.

LYNCH They will.

GRAHAM It's dark now.

(Pause)

LYNCH *(caustically)* So it is.

The street outside the pub

(The camera closes in on the pub doorway as Nicholson stands, looks up and down thoughtfully, lights a cigarette, then walks out of the shot left. Cut to

Tracking shot of Nicholson walking slowly down the street, hands in pockets.)

The C.I.D. room

(*A close shot of Watt on telephone*)

WATT Yes, Bob Stewart, remember him? Breaking and entering, works at night, people not in, on holiday anything like that . . . yes, local lad, went down to the Midlands . . . might be nothing but if you could check round, see if we can tie it in anywhere else . . . thanks . . . yes, I'll be here . . . all night. Aye, let me know. Cheers. (*He puts the receiver down.*)

The Station office

(*Blackitt looks up as Watt enters.*)

BLACKITT Any joy?

WATT They'll be ringing back.

BLACKITT (*yawning*) Roll on morning.

WATT (*brightly*) Morning? You've only just started.

BLACKITT Oh, I'm not complaining, John, don't think that.

WATT Aye, I know . . . flipping heck, that bitter they sell down there, it goes right through you . . . (*he moves to exit.*)

BLACKITT You should give it up.

WATT (*shocked*) Give it up?

BLACKITT Well, you know what they say . . . (*the telephone rings. Blackitt picks up receiver.*) Hello, Newtown Police Station. (*He picks up a pencil.*) Oh, hello, Mr Preston . . .

WATT I'll leave you to it. (*He goes out.*)

BLACKITT I see, he's drunk, you say? . . . not fighting drunk, just quietly aled up, that it?

The pub

(*A close shot of Preston on the telephone continuing the conversation.*)

PRESTON It's a bloke that gets like this occasionally, not regular though, I sometimes take him home myself but the car's in dock . . . Tim Regan, they call him . . .

The Station office

BLACKITT Tim Regan? Yes, I know Tim Regan.

The pub

PRESTON It's just not having the car, exhaust fell off and we need it—having a few days holiday, . . .Hey, you won't arrest him, anything like that? I mean, if you know him, you'll know . . . Ta . . . Yes, not so bad. Thanks.

The Station office

BLACKITT (*on telephone*) Information room, please.
(*Watt enters.*)
WATT Action?
BLACKITT Flying Horse . . . drunk.
WATT Oh.
BLACKITT Tim Regan.
WATT (*reacts*) Tim Regan . . .
BLACKITT Hello, information room . . .

The pub

PRESTON They're sending somebody . . .
ELLIOT Yes, they'll send a car.
PRESTON Hardly like bothering them but . . .
ELLIOT That's what we're there for.
(*Cut to close shot of Regan slumped on bench.*)

The Station office

WATT It's all right, Lynch knows him.
BLACKITT Aye.

The Information Room

(*Close shot of Shirley.*)

SHIRLEY BD to Z Victor Two . . .
(*We hear the distorted voice in reply.*)
GRAHAM Z Victor Two
SHIRLEY Victor Two, go to . . .

A street

(*Z Victor Two parked at kerb in shopping street, Graham in the observer seat. We hear Shirley's message continuing, but distorted now, over the radio.*)
SHIRLEY Flying Horse public house, Newtown. The Landlord, Mr Preston . . .
(*Cut to a long shot looking down the street, over Lynch's shoulder as he is checking shop door, with Z Victor Two framed in long shot.*)

Inside Z Victor Two

GRAHAM Z Victor Two, wilco.
(*Graham replaces receiver, and opens car door.*)

In the street

(*A long shot shooting past Z Victor Two as Graham gets out and whistles through his fingers at Lynch, who comes running.*)

Inside Z Victor Two

(*Graham gets back in, followed, after a pause, by Lynch.*)
LYNCH What's the matter? Somebody been murdered or something?
GRAHAM Fellow got drunk down the Flying Horse.
LYNCH Crime wave.
GRAHAM Little one, just.
LYNCH Any fighting?
GRAHAM Just drunk.

The Station office

BLACKITT Oh yes, he's been going in The Flying Horse for years.
WATT I didn't know how long. (*Pause*) Used to go in . . . like, before?
BLACKITT Stands to reason, doesn't it?

Inside the pub

(*A 2-shot of Mr and Mrs Preston as they tidy away glasses etc.*)
PRESTON They should be here soon.

MRS PRESTON	Don't you wait up if you want to be getting off to bed ...
PRESTON	(*forcefully*) No, I'm all right.
MRS PRESTON	I'll believe you.

(*The camera pans round to Regan, still lying on bench and to a close shot of Elliot standing looking out of the window.*)

The street

(*We see the public house as Z Victor 2 pulls up outside.*)

Inside the pub

(*Elliot who has seen the car*)

ELLIOT	They're here.
PRESTON	Are they? Right.

(*Preston crosses to door to let them in. Lynch and Graham enter. It is obvious that they both know the place, Lynch particularly.*)

LYNCH	Evening, Mr Preston ...
GRAHAM	(*simultaneously*) Evening ...
PRESTON	Hello lads ...
ELLIOT	Good evening.

(*Lynch and Graham are surprised.*)

LYNCH	Terry ...
GRAHAM	Doing a bit of overtime like?
ELLIOT	Not really.
PRESTON	It's Tim Regan.

(*Pause. Lynch walks over to where Regan is lying.*)

PRESTON	Doesn't happen often, not now as much as it used to.
LYNCH	No.
PRESTON	I'd run him home myself but the car's in dock, going away at the weekend and ...
LYNCH	(*to Regan*) C'mon, Dad ... Mr Regan. (*Regan stirs slightly, but hardly seems aware.*) Dave!
GRAHAM	Right.

(*They take a shoulder each and carry Regan to the door.*)

LYNCH	Careful, Dave ...
GRAHAM	Don't fret yourself ...

(*Preston opens door for them. Lynch stands aside to make room.*)

GRAHAM	I'll manage, Bert ...
LYNCH	Sure?

(*Graham nods, exits supporting Regan.*)

ELLIOT	Strong lad, Dave, isn't he?
LYNCH	Eats his rice pudding ... Mr Preston ...

PRESTON Yes . . .

LYNCH I take it there's no formal complaint you wish to make about Mr Regan . . .

PRESTON No, nowt like that . . .

ELLIOT Just that he's drunk, presumably . . . ?

PRESTON No, the thing is, lads, there's no malice in Tim, no malice at all.

LYNCH I know that . . .

PRESTON I'm not trying to do your job, like, but what I mean is you won't . . . you're not going to . . .

LYNCH Leave it with us, Mr Preston.

PRESTON It's just with the car being in dock, I'd run him home myself . . .

LYNCH Just off the Seaport Road, he lives, doesn't he?

PRESTON That's right.

LYNCH Leave it with us . . .

ELLIOT (*sharply*) Bert!

LYNCH Yes, Terry?

PRESTON (*after a pause*) Thanks, lad . . . (*He moves away discreetly.*)

Inside Z Victor Two

(*Graham sits in driver's seat. Regan is in the back. Regan stirs.*)

REGAN No idea, no idea at all . . .

GRAHAM What?

SHIRLEY (*heard over the wireless-telephone*) BD to 146.

REGAN These days, no idea.

GRAHAM (*sighing*) Aye, that's right.
(*Pause*)

REGAN You don't know what I'm on about.

GRAHAM You're right there, Dad.

REGAN (*shaking head*) No idea at all . . . these days.

Inside the pub

ELLIOT (*sharply*) Nothing, I just thought you'd thank me, that's all . . .

LYNCH What for?

ELLIOT For getting you a customer.

LYNCH All right, then . . . thank you.

ELLIOT Has he been up before?

LYNCH What are you talking about?

ELLIOT Regan . . . has he been up for being drunk before?

LYNCH (*precisely*) I don't just remember off-hand. (*Pause*) He might . . . but on the other hand he might not . . . I don't just remember.

ELLIOT   What's the matter with you?

LYNCH   I'm all right, it's the other beggars . . .

ELLIOT   You're not going to take him in, are you?

LYNCH   Er . . . No, I don't think so . . .

ELLIOT   Why not?

LYNCH   (*quietly*) Because . . .

ELLIOT   (*after a pause*) For crying out loud, Bert, I'm not trying to do your job, I just want to know why . . .

LYNCH   (*forcefully*) Right, I'll tell you why. If it hurts. I'm sorry, but you would keep on about it . . .

ELLIOT   Go on . . .

LYNCH   Because this is our patch, we know it . . . we know Tim Regan, we know when he gets tight there's a damn good reason and the best thing we can do is take him home to bed . . . O.K.?

ELLIOT   (*sarcastically*) Of course I'm new around here, I don't know these things.

LYNCH   You said it yourself.

(*Mrs Preston enters.*)

MRS PRESTON   Would you like a drop of something?

LYNCH   No thanks, not for me . . . Better be moving . . .

MRS PRESTON   Well thanks again.

(*Lynch and Mrs Preston move to door.*)

LYNCH   Have a nice holiday.

MRS PRESTON   Thanks, well, I hope it'll . . . maybe do him good, you know . . .

LYNCH   (*quietly*) Aye.

(*Lynch exits. The camera tracks in to a close shot of Elliot's reaction to this apparent understanding between Lynch and the Prestons. He turns to look out of the window as we hear car drive off. Elliot sees something which attracts his attention—something to do with the car.*)

MRS PRESTON   He's a good lad.

ELLIOT   Yes. (*He goes out thoughtfully.*)

Inside Z Victor Two

LYNCH   (*cheerfully to Regan*) All right, Dad?

REGAN   He's a funny feller, this.

GRAHAM   (*quietly*) Home?

LYNCH   Home.

GRAHAM   (*gently*) Drunk and incapable, you can be had up for that, you know.

LYNCH   He's not drunk.

SHIRLEY   (*on the wireless-telephone*) BD to 146.

GRAHAM   (*sceptically*) Isn't he?

LYNCH   Just a bit off-colour.

REGAN Did you hear that? One four six.

GRAHAM Off colour, you reckon?

LYNCH I know the way.

(*Graham starts the car, and they move off.*)

GRAHAM You can make the report out.

REGAN Treble eighteen, treble twenty, pair of sixteens ... (*pause*) Good finish.

LYNCH You'll have done that a few times, Dad.

REGAN A few times. (*Pause*) He's a funny feller, that mate of yours.

LYNCH (*smiling*) There's a few funny fellers about.

Another street in Newtown

(*A medium shot of a fish-and-chip shop, tracking in slowly to the doorway as Nicholson emerges with a packet. He stops to open it. We cut to a different angle, shooting down the street with Nicholson in the foreground, eating his fish and chips as the Beat Constable walks past. There is no reaction from Nicholson.*)

Inside Z Victor Two

LYNCH Next on the left, Dave.

GRAHAM (*after a pause*) That's what you told Elliot?

LYNCH Aye.

GRAHAM I only hope you're right, that's all.

LYNCH Have you ever known me be wrong?

GRAHAM I never spoke.

REGAN Next on the left, tell your mate.

A side street in Newtown

(*A medium shot of Z Victor Two as it turns into the side-street. Cut to a close shot of Z Victor Two as it parks in front of a large, decaying Victorian house. Lynch gets out and opens the door for Regan. Lynch helps him out. Cut to a shot across the bonnet of the car towards the house as Lynch and Regan walk across to the front door. Regan opens door.*)

Inside Z Victor Two

(*We see a close shot of Graham's reaction. He is doubtful whether Lynch is doing the right thing.*)

Inside the hallway of Regan's house

(*Lynch and Regan enter.*)

LYNCH   Up the stairs, is it?

REGAN   Down the passage, now.

LYNCH   Saves you climbing.

REGAN   That's what I always reckon.

(They walk down the passage at the side of staircase.)

Inside Regan's room

(It is a small, shabbily furnished and not particularly clean bedsitter. Lynch and Regan enter.)

REGAN   Not very ... like, not much to look at but ... nobody comes much, as a rule.

(He lights a small gas ring and puts the kettle on.)

The C.I.D. office

(Watt is on the telephone.)

WATT   He did? Good ... aye, just this fellow in the pub, I overheard him saying ... yes ... well, it passes the night away ... yes, very quiet ... unnatural ... see you!

(He puts the receiver down and walks into the station office.)

The Station office

(Watt enters.)

WATT   I was right, Blackie ...

BLACKITT   *(blankly)* Good.

WATT   Spot on.

BLACKITT   I'm glad about that.

WATT   *(realising that Blackitt has not understood)* About Bob Stewart.

BLACKITT   *(as the truth dawns)* Oh.

WATT   They've had a good check round ... looks like he's been busy in Seaport, and the Pool, and a few other places ... they just found a fingerprint this afternoon.

BLACKITT   Oh aye. Sixteen points of resemblance?

WATT   *(picking up phone)* Information room please ... *(to Blackitt)* about fourteen and a half ...

Inside Regan's room

(Regan is sitting in an armchair. Lynch stands.)

REGAN   Funny, what you said, in the car.

LYNCH   Did I say something?

REGAN   He's not drunk, he's just off-colour.

LYNCH It's . . . figure of speech.
REGAN It's my arm, you know, lot of trouble with my arm . . .

Inside Z Victor Two

(*Graham sits, looking towards the house. He is a little impatient.*)

Inside Regan's room

REGAN That was the start of . . .
LYNCH I know it was, Dad.
REGAN The end, more like . . .
LYNCH How about getting yourself to bed? Good night's sleep . . .
REGAN Kettle's boiling. (*He goes across to the kettle to make tea.*)

The Information Room

SHIRLEY BD to Z Victor Two, keep a lookout for Robert Stewart, believed
to be in the Newtown or Seaport area . . .

Inside Z Victor Two

(*Graham is listening to the message.*)
SHIRLEY (*distort*) Wanted for questioning in connection with housebreaking
in Seaport and . . .

Regan's room

REGAN Will you have a cup?
LYNCH No thanks, I've got work to do, my mate's outside.
REGAN Funny feller, that.
LYNCH You get used to people.

REGAN   I've set you a cup.

LYNCH   Another time, maybe but . . .

REGAN   Your mate's outside.

LYNCH   Aye.

REGAN   (*sharply*) What you hanging about for then?
         (*Lynch moves to door.*)

LYNCH   Goodnight' Dad.

REGAN   Evening.
         (*Lynch exits.*)

Inside Z Victor Two

GRAHAM   Z Victor Two to BD, wilco.
         (*Graham puts the receiver down and looks across to house. He sees Lynch, who is just coming. Lynch gets in.*)

GRAHAM   I thought you were stopping the night.

LYNCH   He wanted me to have a cup of tea with him.

GRAHAM   You've had time for a knife and fork do.

LYNCH   (*sharply*) And what of it?

GRAHAM   Nowt really. (*Pause: handing him pad.*) We've got to find him.

LYNCH   (*looking at the message on the pad*) Easy.

Inside Regan's room

(*Regan is sitting at the table. There is a teapot, bottle of milk, two battered cups, a packet of sugar, half torn off. He pours out one cup of tea.*)

The street in Newtown near the fish-and-chip shop.

(*Nicholson bundles the fish-and-chip paper into a ball, and is about to put it in a wastepaper box on the lampstandard, then changes his mind. He tosses it in the air, and catches it. Drops it on the ground and kicks it along the pavement. We cut to a low angle shot as Nicholson dribbles the 'ball', hands in pockets, into the camera.*)

Inside Z Victor Two

LYNCH They call that a description?

GRAHAM Get a photograph tomorrow, likely.

LYNCH There's hundreds of ordinary, middle-aged blokes like that ... all in bed by now ...

GRAHAM Stewart an' all, I shouldn't wonder.

LYNCH I think Blackie's mentioned him ... think he works nights ... unless I'm thinking of someone else, Blackie knows them all ...

GRAHAM Aye. ... Look at them all!

A street in Newtown

(*A long shot of Z Victor Two as it cruises down a deserted street.*)

Inside Z Victor Two

LYNCH What?

GRAHAM Hundreds of middle-aged burglars ...

LYNCH Oh, give over ...

GRAHAM You don't mean to say you missed them!

LYNCH It's late, you're getting delirious ...

GRAHAM I'll start singing in a minute.

LYNCH You don't mind if I walk, Dave?

GRAHAM You didn't hear me in Gilbert and Sullivan, when I was at school ...

LYNCH No, I'm glad to say ...

GRAHAM You missed a treat, I'll tell you, I ... (*He breaks off as he sees something.*) Hold on, Bert, anchors!

A street in Newtown

(*A medium long shot of Z Victor Two as it brakes sharply, just after passing a back entry to some houses.*)

Inside Z Victor Two

LYNCH What the Hell do you think ... ?

GRAHAM That back entry, there's a car down there ...

LYNCH There isn't, as a rule ...

GRAHAM Smart lad, Bert. (*He puts a hand on the door handle.*)

LYNCH No, Dave. Drive up it, block the way out.

The street

(*Z Victor Two reverses quickly along street, then turns into the back entry. Cut to a high angle shot as Z Victor Two drives into the back entry, headlights on, stops. Lynch gets out and walks to the parked car.*)

Inside Z Victor Two

(*We see Graham watching carefully, ready to get out if necessary. After a pause he relaxes and smiles. Lynch returns and gets into car.*)

GRAHAM Spoil-sport.

LYNCH She was all right.

GRAHAM Can't leave it alone, some people.

LYNCH Bad for public relations though, Dave . . .

GRAHAM Aye, but you've got to check.

LYNCH Oh, I did, I asked to see his licence.

GRAHAM Eh? You don't need a licence for *that*. (*He prepares to back out.*)

LYNCH Oh . . . careful how you go, Dave; we don't want another bump . . .

GRAHAM (*aghast*) You what?

The street

(*Z Victor Two reverses out of the back entry and stops. The camera zooms in for a close shot of the front wing, which has a small but noticeable bump.*)

Inside Station office

BLACKITT (*at desk*) Lads'll be in in ten minutes.

WATT (*reading a paper*) Lot of money for a goalkeeper.

BLACKITT I'll get kettle on . . . (*he stands up.*)

WATT I said it's a lot of money . . .

BLACKITT Aye, it is . . . for a goalkeeper . . .

WATT (*after a pause*) Get the kettle on, Blackie . . .

Inside Z Victor Two

(*The car is still. Lynch is sitting in the observer seat watching Graham, who is inspecting the bump. Graham gets in.*)

GRAHAM Well it wasn't us . . .

LYNCH I never said it was . . .

GRAHAM Hey . . . Jock and Fancy had the car this afternoon, didn't they?

LYNCH The thought had crossed my mind . . .

GRAHAM Aye . . . well I mean, it's not bad really . . . shows up a bit, all the same . . .

LYNCH Fancy never said anything, did he?

GRAHAM Not a dickey bird . . .

LYNCH Thing is . . . is it an official bump or an unofficial bump?

GRAHAM Nowt's been said . . . (*Pause*) Unofficial.

LYNCH All seems a bit unofficial to me . . .
(*Pause. Graham drives off slowly.*)

GRAHAM Bet you a dollar it was Fancy Smith . . .

LYNCH More than likely.

GRAHAM It's them great clod-hopping feet of his . . .

LYNCH Listen to him!

GRAHAM Well I'm not carrying the can 'cause Fancy takes a liking to somebody's gatepost . . .

LYNCH (*after a pause*) A bit of discretion, that's what's called for . . .

GRAHAM Little job for Jimmy Oliver?

LYNCH He's been a good friend to us, Jimmy . . .

GRAHAM Open all night, isn't he?

LYNCH Straight after we've had tea.

A street

(*Nicholson sits down on a bench at the street corner. The camera tracks in for a close shot as he lights a cigarette, looking up and down the street a little nervously as he tosses the match away.*)

Inside Z Victor Two

LYNCH (*sighing*) It's all go, isn't it?

GRAHAM Bert.

LYNCH I said, it's all go. Eh?

GRAHAM That fellow we took home, before, Regan, wasn't it?

LYNCH What about him?

GRAHAM I keep thinking . . . like, I'm not trying to pick a fight but . . . well, you get an old soak like him, maybe take him in . . . just once.

LYNCH Give him a fright?

GRAHAM Aye. Course, Regan, good old Irish name, isn't it?

LYNCH Feel a bit sorry for him, he had . . . something happen, when he was in the pits.

GRAHAM How do you mean?

LYNCH Got his arm crushed, had to pack the job in . . .

GRAHAM I know, Bert, it's hard luck but plenty other blokes get hurt . . . plenty blokes, they don't drink themselves daft every night . . .

LYNCH It wasn't just the job.

GRAHAM What then? (*There is a pause.*) Bert?
(*Lynch is searching the car.*)

47

LYNCH   Have you seen my gloves, Dave?
GRAHAM   Gloves?

The Station office

(*Blackitt is on the telephone, being very polite. Watt is watching, smiling.*)
BLACKITT   Yes sir, playing football, I see ... in Freehold Street, a middle-aged man you said? ... yes, and he didn't appear to be drunk. Was it a ... real football he was using? ... Rolled up newspapers, I see ... pardon? Oh yes, dribbling it. Well, there's nothing illegal in doing this but ... Oh, I quite agree, extremely suspicious, quite right to report it. (*He makes face at Watt who is very amused.*) Yes, we'll give it our immediate attention, sir ... thank you, good night. (*He puts the phone down.*) Councillor Purvis.
WATT   Very public-spirited.
BLACKITT   Seen this fellow dribbling a bundle of newspapers down the street, couldn't sleep for worrying about it.
WATT   (*deadpan*) Serious, John, there's been a lot of dribbling round here lately.
BLACKITT   Councillors! I've shot 'em.
WATT   He'll check up on it, you know.
BLACKITT   I'll have an answer for him, John.

Inside Z Victor Two

LYNCH   That's the second pair, Dave.
GRAHAM   Whose fault is it?
LYNCH   The second pair this year.
GRAHAM   We'll club together.
LYNCH   Don't be stupid!
GRAHAM   I'll get me mam to knit you some woolly mitts.
   (*Lynch does not react.*)
GRAHAM   I'll make you a cup of tea.
LYNCH   Thanks.

The street

(*Nicholson is trying to sleep on the bench. He stirs, trying to get comfortable, then sits up, stiffly. He looks up and down the street. He looks worried. We cut to a long shot from Nicholson's point of view of the beat constable approaching. Cut to a close shot of Nicholson's reaction. Cut to a medium long shot of Nicholson as he gets up and walks quietly on, turning round corner and out of shot. Cut to a low-angle tracking shot of the policeman's legs.*)

The Station office

(*Lynch and Graham have returned.*)

LYNCH   You're sure you haven't seen any lying around?

BLACKITT   Sorry, Bert, got most things but I'm right out of gloves.

LYNCH   Blast!

BLACKITT   I've boiled kettle for you.

WATT   He's a smart lad, Bobby Stewart.

GRAHAM   He'll have to be, won't he?

LYNCH   Twice this year, you know that?

BLACKITT   Sheer carelessness.

WATT   He's quite liable to see you before you see him.

GRAHAM   Won't see him tonight, any road. Dead quiet it is.

WATT   Aye, (*He exits to the C.I.D. room.*)

GRAHAM   (*to Lynch*) Coming?

LYNCH   What?

BLACKITT   Hang on, lads . . .

GRAHAM   Eh?

BLACKITT   Just wondering . . . what's going on between you two and Fancy Smith?

GRAHAM   Fancy Smith?

LYNCH   What's it all about, sarge?

BLACKITT   There's something going on, that's all . . . Just after you went on duty, in comes Fancy, dead worried he was . . . 'Where's Bert?' he says, 'Where's Dave?'

GRAHAM   He said that?

BLACKITT   'I want to see them' . . . dead worried. Couldn't weigh it up at all . . .

LYNCH   Very mysterious . . .

BLACKITT   (*to Graham*) I mean, who'd want to see Bert Lynch?

LYNCH   You'd be surprised.

BLACKITT   What's it all about then?

LYNCH   No idea. That right, Dave? No idea.

GRAHAM   No.

BLACKITT   Well Fancy wasn't cracking on . . .

GRAHAM   Aye.

BLACKITT   You what?

LYNCH   We weren't going to tell you but seeing as you've guessed . . . Fancy Smith left a bomb in the car . . .

BLACKITT   It's amazing what some people'll do, isn't it?

(*Watt returns from the C.I.D. room, with a serious expression.*)

WATT   By the way lads . . . you did hear about Mr Barlow . . . ?

LYNCH   No, what about him?

WATT (*serious*) Found at Newtown cross-roads, half an hour ago, stark naked except . . .

LYNCH Except for his helmet . . .

WATT You heard about it.

GRAHAM Yes, we heard about it.

WATT Better go and have a cup of tea then, hadn't you?
(*Lynch and Graham exit.*)

WATT Funny lads . . .

BLACKITT Aye. Funny.

The shopping centre of Newtown

(*A medium long shot of the clock on upper storey of a shop showing two a.m., then pan down to a doorway as Nicholson walks along and into doorway. Cut to a closer shot of Nicholson as he takes out cigarette, puts it in his mouth. He takes out matches but the box is empty. He throws box away, shrugs, and moves out of the doorway. Cut to a long shot, looking along the street, as Nicholson walks slowly away from the camera, then pan down to the match-box lying on the pavement.*)

Inside Z Victor Two

(*The car is outside the police station. Lynch and Graham get in the driver's seat.*)

LYNCH (*sighing*) Home again.

GRAHAM First five years are the worst, they reckon.

LYNCH Depends on the company you keep.
(*They drive off in silence.*)

GRAHAM Coming in a bit sharp now.

LYNCH (*after a pause*) That's right.

GRAHAM Oh aye. No gloves.

LYNCH (*after another pause*) That's right.

GRAHAM Rough, isn't it? (*He pauses*) Anyhow, we know now.

LYNCH Know what?

GRAHAM That bump. It's unofficial.

LYNCH Blackie going on like that, he knew something was up . . . made me feel a right Charlie . . .

GRAHAM I was right, any road . . .

LYNCH About what?

GRAHAM Fancy Smith, that's who did it . . .

LYNCH Yes, I'll be having a word with him in the morning . . .

GRAHAM Straight on, isn't it? Jimmy Oliver's garage?

LYNCH (*sarcastically*) Where do you think I'm going?

GRAHAM (*shrugs*) Thought you were looking for your gloves.

The Station office

(*Watt and Blackitt are having a cup of tea and swopping jokes.*)
WATT Disgusting!
BLACKITT So he says 'Blow it, I'll walk'.
WATT Spreading stuff like that, fellow of your age.
BLACKITT It's people like you, encouraging me . . .

A street in Newtown

(*Nicholson is sheltering in a shop doorway, feeling the cold. Z Victor Two cruises past.*)

Inside Z Victor Two

GRAHAM (*urgently*) Bert!
LYNCH What?
GRAHAM Bloke in Jackson's doorway.
LYNCH Right!

A street

(*Z Victor Two reverses up the street, turns round in reverse so that it faces the doorway. From the door of the shop we see Z Victor Two drive up, head-lights on. Nicholson runs from doorway. Graham gets out of the car and runs after Nicholson, who stops. We see a close shot of Nicholson.*)

NICHOLSON What's up?
GRAHAM Bit late to be hanging round isn't it?
NICHOLSON Aye, a bit late.
(*Graham and Nicholson turn and walk slowly towards car.*)

Inside Z Victor Two

(*Graham and Nicholson get in. Nicholson is in the front seat between Graham and Lynch.*)
NICHOLSON (*to Lynch*) Cold . . . tonight.
LYNCH Haven't you got a home to go to?
NICHOLSON Well, yes, course I have, only . . .
GRAHAM Lost your front door key?
NICHOLSON No, I've got my key. I think it's . . . (*he searches*) . . . here, got my key look . . .
LYNCH You should go home where it's warm.

51

NICHOLSON Well . . .
LYNCH Mr Stewart, is it?
NICHOLSON Nicholson.
LYNCH Are you sure?
NICHOLSON Course I'm bloody sure!

Inside the C.I.D. room

WATT (*on telephone*) Yes, Sergeant Watt speaking . . . have they? Manchester? . . . No, they're welcome, this is a respectable parish . . .

Inside Z Victor Two

NICHOLSON No, Nicholson! Look, see, I've got the key but the door's bolted as well.
LYNCH And there's nobody in.
NICHOLSON That's right.
LYNCH Except the person that bolted the door.
NICHOLSON Ah.
LYNCH Ah.
GRAHAM Have another go.
SHIRLEY (*whose voice is heard, distorted, over the wireless*) BD to Z Victor Two.
GRAHAM Z Victor Two.

The Information Room

SHIRLEY (*continuing*) Cancel previous instructions regarding Robert Stewart, the suspect is now in police custody. (*There is a pause.*) Z Victor Two, please acknowledge.

Inside Z Victor Two

GRAHAM Z Victor Two, wilco.

NICHOLSON (*after a pause*) Stewart, she said.

LYNCH Where do you live, Mr Nicholson?

The Station office

(*Watt is telling Blackitt the news.*)

BLACKITT They got him?

WATT Foot patrol in Manchester, found him halfway through the bog window, back of an off-licence.

BLACKITT Lads'll be able to relax, then.

WATT What, Lynch and Graham? Aye. (*He pauses*) Hundred-and-fifty stolen cars to be looking for, help them pass the time.

BLACKITT Unless 'owt happens.

WATT I suppose it could. Late though.

Inside Z Victor Two

(*Nicholson is now in the back seat.*)

NICHOLSON Not that I blame her, I don't blame her ... it's nasty, what I done.

LYNCH Good-looking typist, you'll not be the first.

NICHOLSON At my age an' all. Stupid.

GRAHAM Your wife, like, slung you out?

NICHOLSON Bolted the door.

LYNCH Have you got a back door key?

(*Pause*)

NICHOLSON Yes. I've got a back door key.

GRAHAM Has she bolted the back door as well?

NICHOLSON (*hesitating*) No.

GRAHAM Well, what ... like, why don't you ... ?

LYNCH Why didn't you go home?

NICHOLSON Stupid. Don't laugh, will you? It's just I thought I might ... like it, not going home, thought I might like it.

LYNCH You mean freedom?

NICHOLSON I thought I might but it's stupid, at my age ... you only look a fool. And you feel the cold as well, and I didn't know what to do ... where to go, and I said to her, I'm not coming back and I thought I might like it. Don't laugh.

(*They drive on a little.*)

LYNCH Is this it?

NICHOLSON Yes ... Drop me here, I'll walk ... round the back.

LYNCH   Right.

A residential street in Newtown

(Z Victor Two pulls up and Nicholson gets out. Z Victor Two moves on. Close shot of Nicholson, watching the car drive off. Cut to a long shot of the street as Nicholson stands, quite still, looking at his house.)

Inside Z Victor Two

(Lynch and Graham are both smiling.)

GRAHAM   You've met 'em.

LYNCH   It's a woman's world, Dave.

GRAHAM   Be rotten without them, I'll say that.

LYNCH   Sometimes it's rotten with 'em . . .

GRAHAM   You can't kid me.

LYNCH   Just because I sometimes go out with girls . . .

GRAHAM   *(scornful)* Girls! That what you call them? What about Edna?

LYNCH   Just watch it, Graham! *(He aims a blow at Graham.)*

GRAHAM   Steady Bert, who's driving?
           (They continue for a few moments.)

GRAHAM   Let's get that bump straightened out before anything else happens . . .

Inside the Station office

BLACKITT   Just rang through.

WATT   They did what?

BLACKITT   Picked this feller up, thought it might be Stewart, description tallied, like. Turned out he'd got slung out by his missus, been larking about with some judy from work.

WATT   What they do? Send him home?

BLACKITT   Not much else they could do, really. *(Lightheartedly)* Bet he got a loving reception.

WATT   Aye, well there's two sides to it, Blackie . . .

BLACKITT   Yes. *(Pause)* Sorry John.

WATT   Oh, it's nowt to do with you. Best not to laugh though. *(He moves to door of C.I.D. office.)* It helps, working these God-awful hours. Fills the time. *(He exits.)*

Outside a garage and service station

(Z Victor Two turns off the main road and drives into garage.)

Inside the garage

(*We see a small office adjoining the main garage area—not too tidy, littered with tools and bits of cars. Lynch, Graham, and Oliver enter. Oliver is a big, robust man in his early fifties.*)

OLIVER Well I thought you'd be in earlier ...

LYNCH Earlier?

OLIVER That mate of yours, he told me you wanted it straightening out ... you know, the big feller ...

GRAHAM Fancy Smith ...

OLIVER Aye, Fancy ... he said he'd tell you ...

LYNCH He said that, did he?

OLIVER Funny lad that Fancy ...

GRAHAM Very funny.

OLIVER Anyhow, Jack'll have it tidied up in no time. It's nowt much to fret about ... here ... (*He hands his cigarettes round.*)

LYNCH Ta.

OLIVER Keeping busy then?

GRAHAM No. Very quiet. Hey, can we hear if there's any calls come through?

OLIVER Don't worry, Jack'll give you the aye aye ...

GRAHAM Ah.

LYNCH We put Freddie Bishop and his gang away for three months ... Its keeping the rest of them in their holes ...

OLIVER Good riddance ... they were sizing this place up, you know, well I told you ... didn't I?

GRAHAM That's right.

OLIVER Just one long holiday then, is it?

GRAHAM Found one bloke tonight running away, sick of his missus ...

OLIVER Did he look like me?

GRAHAM Not really ... anyway, we reunited them ...

OLIVER Makes you feel warm inside doesn't it?

LYNCH And we took Tim Regan home, been hitting it again ...

OLIVER Tim?

GRAHAM You know him?

OLIVER Oh aye, I know Tim ... poor bastard.

A small bed-sitting room

(*Mrs French, grey-haired lady in her sixties, is looking for her shoes. She wears a rather shabby raincoat apparently serving as a dressing gown. The room is a bedsitter, furnished saleroom fashion, with a great many additions bearing Mrs French's hand-photographs, bits of pottery, china ornaments, etc. She finds a pair of slippers and puts them on.*)

The garage office

OLIVER Well, he smashed his right arm, you see, had to pack his job in . . .

GRAHAM Bert told me about that.

OLIVER But it was his right arm, you see . . .

GRAHAM (*obviously not seeing any importance in this fact*) Oh. His right arm.

Mrs French's bedroom

(*Mrs French is rummaging in her handbag. She finds her purse, slips it in her pocket, and exits.*)

The garage office

OLIVER Best flaming darts player you ever saw, kid, I'm telling you . . .

GRAHAM (*suddenly realising*) Darts . . . I'm with you now . . .

The C.I.D. office

(*Watt is going through some papers carefully.*)

The Station office

(*Blackitt is reading the paper, almost dozing off.*)

The garage office

OLIVER Best player in the district, dozens of cups he must have won . . .

GRAHAM Broke him up, like, when he couldn't play any more?

OLIVER Sits in The Flying Horse, night after night, telling everybody else how to play . . .

LYNCH   I've heard him many a time . . .

GRAHAM   Can't he play at all now?

OLIVER   Used to try sometimes but he could hardly hit the wall . . .

GRAHAM   Ah.

OLIVER   Doesn't bother any more . . . sort of . . . embarrassing . . .

GRAHAM   (*after a pause*) Aye, it's rough on a bloke, owt like that . . .

OLIVER   I mean, it's years ago but . . . suppose it ruined his life really . . . used to play with him myself, always beat me, like . . . when I was your age . . .

LYNCH   I know, when I took him home he . . .

OLIVER   Tell you who else used to play, them days . . . Blackie, you know your feller . . .

GRAHAM   Sergeant Blackitt . . .

OLIVER   Aye, Blackie, that's what we always called him . . .

GRAHAM   Still do . . .

LYNCH   When I took him home, Regan I mean . . . went in with him and . . . he was dead eager for me to have a cup of tea with him . . .

GRAHAM   You said.

LYNCH   Did I?

GRAHAM   You said.

OLIVER   Aye . . . maybe Jack'll have that car straightened out by now . . . (*He exits*)

The Station office

(*Blackitt folds up the newspaper, and puts it in the drawer. He yawns and looks at his watch.*)

The C.I.D. office

(*Watt looks briefly at his watch. Then continues working.*)

A street in Newtown

(*Mrs French is making way nervously down the dark street.*)

The Station office

(*Blackitt moves across to the door of the c.i.d. office and opens it.*)

BLACKITT Will you look after the desk, John? Five minutes?

(*Watt comes out into the station office.*)

WATT Expecting a big rush?

BLACKITT Efficiency, John.

WATT Where you off to?

BLACKITT It's a long night.

A street in Newtown

(*Mrs French is going into a telephone kiosk at the street corner.*)

Inside the telephone kiosk

(*Mrs French is struggling, without her glasses, to read the instructions in the directory.*)

Inside Z Victor Two

GRAHAM Twenty minutes.

LYNCH Roll on breakfast.

GRAHAM Made a good job of that wing, did Jimmy . . .

LYNCH One good turn deserves . . .

GRAHAM I know. Touched it up an' all, where it was scratched, that last time . . .

LYNCH My guts are making terrible noises . . .

GRAHAM Good. I thought it was me. (*Pause*) Do you fancy the canal bank? Bit of rat catching?

LYNCH Not in the mood for blood sports . . .

GRAHAM (*looking out*) By heck, they're sleeping sound tonight . . .

LYNCH They'll be getting up soon. (*Pause*) If you want something to do, look for my gloves . . .

The Station office

(*Watt is at the desk as Blackitt returns.*)

BLACKITT Busy?

WATT I've never stopped.

BLACKITT Keeps you young. This time of night, your flaming watch stands still . . .

WATT Yes, I know, it always . . .

(The telephone rings.)

BLACKITT Hello, Newtown Police Station . . . who's speaking please . . . Mrs French? *(To Watt)* Mrs French.

WATT Mrs French and Councillor Purvis, all in one night!

The telephone kiosk

RS FRENCH Mr Blackitt, is that Mr Blackitt? It's happened again, Mr Blackitt . . .

The Station office

BLACKITT *(patiently)* Can you give me a few details, Mrs French? Where are you speaking from? . . . I see . . . and . . .

The telephone kiosk

RS FRENCH It's the main, you see, it's the main, they had the road up only last month, fellows from council came and dug it up . . . yes, the main . .

The Station office

BLACKITT The main. *(To Watt)* She's smelling things again.

WATT Again?

BLACKITT All right, Mrs French, you just pop along home and we'll send somebody straight away . . . pardon? Right, we'll send somebody to the call-box . . . *(To Watt)* late, frightened of the dark . . . That's all right, don't worry . . . five minutes.

(He puts phone down.)

WATT She's a good smeller, that one.

BLACKITT I should say so, had the fire brigade out last year, people next door singed their bacon . . . *(He picks up the telephone.)* Information room.

Inside Z Victor Two

GRAHAM Ten minutes.

LYNCH I still haven't found my gloves.

(There is a pause)

LYNCH *(defensively)* It's annoying, a thing like that.

GRAHAM I know.
(*Another pause*)
GRAHAM How about a last drag?
LYNCH (*shrugs*) If you like . . .
SHIRLEY (*over the wireless*) BD to Z Victor Two.
(*Graham and Lynch look at each other.*)
GRAHAM (*answering*) Z Victor Two.

The Information Room

SHIRLEY Go immediately to public telephone box, Richmond Terrace, Newtown. See Mrs French about a reported gas leak.
GRAHAM (*heard over the wireless*) Z Victor Two, wilco.

Inside Z Victor Two

GRAHAM Line of duty, Bert.
LYNCH Line of duty, Dave.

The Station office

BLACKITT They'll be dead chuffed about that . . . ten to . . .
WATT Makes them feel wanted.

The street in Newtown

(*Mrs French waiting outside telephone kiosk, a little impatiently.*)

Inside Z Victor Two

LYNCH (*scornfully*) They never did!
GRAHAM Honest, Bert. Up in the flats on the estate, this bloke he'd dragged

himself out on to the landing . . . room full of gas . . .

LYNCH Aye.

GRAHAM And some of the locals thought he was tight, and they dragged him back in again, left him there.

LYNCH Was he all right?

GRAHAM One of the lads got involved, bit of a fight started, see, so they got him out, like . . . only just.

LYNCH The things they do, the English.

(*A pause as they come to the telephone box.*)

GRAHAM That must be her.

LYNCH She's the sort that smells gas.

The street in Newtown

(*Z Victor Two drives up and pulls into kerbside. Graham gets out.*)

GRAHAM Mrs French?

MRS FRENCH What kept you?

(*Graham opens back door and she gets in; Graham also gets in.*)

Inside Z Victor Two

MRS FRENCH It's only about hundred yards, on the right . . . it's the main . . .

LYNCH Right. (*He drives off.*)

MRS FRENCH It's dark, see, I get a bit nervous . . . next on the right.

LYNCH Near where Tim Regan lives.

MRS FRENCH Yes, Mr Regan's got the room under mine.

LYNCH (*quietly*) Jesus!

Outside Regan's house

(*Z Victor Two pulls up. Lynch and Graham get out and run to the front door, which is unlocked.*)

Inside the hallway

(*Lynch rushes in, followed by Graham. Lynch moves down the passage to Regan's room.*)

GRAHAM Careful, Bert . . .

LYNCH Sure I'll be careful . . . (*He opens door of Regan's room.*) Ambulance, Dave! And a doctor . . .

(*Lynch goes in and there is a crash as he breaks the window. Graham exits. Neighbours drift into the hallway, attracted by noise. Simpson, a dowdy ex-military man, in pajamas and dressing gown, sees Mrs French come in.*)

C

SIMPSON What's happening?

MRS FRENCH I thought it was the main.

Inside Z Victor Two

GRAHAM Z Victor Two to BD, emergency! (*Pause*) Z Victor Two to BD emergency!

SHIRLEY (*heard over the wireless*) Z Victor Two.

GRAHAM Re your last message, will you send an ambulance, immediately to . . .

Inside the hallway

(*Lynch, coughing, is carrying Regan out into the hallway.*)

LYNCH Open the door! Let's have some air!

(*Mrs French does so.*)

LYNCH Is there a doctor near here?

SIMPSON There's Doctor Nelson in Afton Street, that's not too . . .

LYNCH Go and get him!

SIMPSON I'm in my pajamas.

LYNCH Take them off then!

Inside Z Victor Two.

GRAHAM (*speaking urgently over the wireless telephone*) Regan, Timothy Regan

The Station office

BLACKITT (*on phone*) Right. (*He puts the phone down.*) Tim Regan.

WATT What about him?

BLACKITT Found him . . . gassed.

WATT Done it himself? (*Blackitt shrugs.*) Well, did they . . . were they . . .?

The Information Room

SHIRLEY BD to Z Victor Two (*pause*) BD to Z Victor Two.

Inside Z Victor Two

(*Graham gets in leaving the door open. He leans across to pick up the receiver.*)

GRAHAM Z Victor Two . . .

SHIRLEY An ambulance is on its way, do you require a doctor?

GRAHAM No thanks; we've got a doctor . . .

The Station office

WATT What I mean is, *if* he has . . .

BLACKITT You can't tell.

WATT But *if*. . . I mean, it wouldn't be a surprise.

BLACKITT You can't tell.

Outside the house

(*A medium long shot of the house as the ambulance drives up. Cut to closer shot as the ambulance men get out and are met by Graham and taken into the house.*)

The Information Room

(*Shirley is tidying the desk. She collects things into her handbag, runs comb through her hair, gets up, and exits.*)

The Station office

(*Watt and Blackitt nod as two constables come in.*)

WATT Think I'll hang on.

BLACKITT Aye.

Outside the house

(*The ambulance men carry a stretcher down the path and into the ambulance, very slowly and carefully.*)

Inside the hallway

DOCTOR Rather too late, I'm afraid.

GRAHAM (*nodding*) Thanks for turning out.

DOCTOR I'll be hearing from you . . .

GRAHAM Yes . . . (*He sees Simpson still in his pajamas. To Simpson*) Thanks. (*Graham looks round for Lynch.*)

The Station office

(*Watt has his coat and hat on. Blackitt is putting his coat on.*)

BLACKITT Lovely player, in his prime.

WATT I never saw him play.

BLACKITT Made it look easy.

Inside Regan's room

(*A close shot of the table. There are two cups of tea poured out. Then the camera pans up to Lynch's face.*)

LYNCH He poured me a cup, Dave. (*There is a pause.*)

GRAHAM Coming, Bert?

LYNCH We've finished for the night, haven't we?

GRAHAM Half an hour ago.

LYNCH (*after another pause*) He wanted me to . . . have a . . .

GRAHAM You said.

(*Lynch and Graham move out of the room.*)

Inside the hallway

(*Lynch and Graham walk through Regan's door into the hall.*)

GRAHAM	I've found your gloves . . .
LYNCH	Gloves?
GRAHAM	You'd left them on the hallstand . . . before . . .
	(*He hands Lynch his gloves.*)
LYNCH	Good.
	(*They exit.*)

The police canteen the next morning

(*Haywood and Freda are at counter. Freda is a down-to-earth working mum serving behind the counter. Haywood is collecting his bacon and eggs.*)

FREDA	All right, love?
HAYWOOD	Fine, thanks. Hey, did you hear about Mr Barlow?
FREDA	Mr Barlow, what about him?
HAYWOOD	Standing at Newtown crossroads, middle of the night, stark naked . . .
FREDA	Give over, girl of my age . . .
	(*Cut to Lynch and Graham sitting at a table. Elliot joins them.*)
ELLIOT	Have a good night then?
GRAHAM	Quiet.
ELLIOT	Good. (*He pauses*) I hear you had a gassing.
	(*Lynch gets up and crosses to counter.*)
ELLIOT	What's the matter?
GRAHAM	It's the smell of gas . . . he's allergic . . .
ELLIOT	Hey, Dave, something else I noticed . . .
GRAHAM	What's that then?
ELLIOT	When you came to the pub last night . . . spotted it, bump on the front wing of the car . . .
GRAHAM	A bump?
ELLIOT	Nearside, front . . .
GRAHAM	You must be thinking of some other car . . . no bumps on Z Victor Two . . .
ELLIOT	Come on, Dave, I saw it . . .
GRAHAM	Have a look then.
ELLIOT	You've had it fixed?
GRAHAM	Don't be daft! In the middle of the night?
	(*Cut to Lynch, Haywood, and Freda at the counter.*)
HAYWOOD	In the middle of the night, with just his helmet on . . .
FREDA	What's it to be Bert?
LYNCH	Cup of tea, please.
HAYWOOD	Directing the traffic . . .
FREDA	Nothing to eat?
HAYWOOD	Anyhow, up comes Mr Robins and . . .

LYNCH No thanks.

FREDA Sure?

LYNCH (*sharply*) A cup of tea!

(*They look at him as the picture fades. The screen is filled with a close up of Regan's table, as before, with two cups of tea poured out.*)

Window Dressing by Ronald Eyre

The Cast

Detective Chief Inspector Barlow
Detective Sergeant Watt
Sergeant Blackitt
PC David Graham
PC Baker
PC Taylor
Girl on duty in the Information Room
Terry Greenhalgh, a youth of about seventeen
Gordon Plimmer, of about the same age
Mrs Greenhalgh, Terry's mother
Mr Greenhalgh, his father
Mr Aspin, the Probation Officer
Mr Mercer, owner of *Mercer's Universal Stores*
The Senior Assistant at Mercer's store
Mr Heaversedge, who runs the garage at which Plimmer
    works
Molloy, a cafe-owner
Carroll, an elderly Irishman
Sampson, a university student
A photographer from the local paper
A youth at the probation office

Shop assistants, customers in the cafe, youths in the
    amusement arcade

Window Dressing

A roof-top by night

(We see the flat roof of a largish block of flats. A sky-light is open, and we hear the sound of climbing up the ladder to the sky-light, from inside. They're having trouble. Bumps and knocks. Off the screen, we hear two voices.)

GREEN-
HALGH   Damn. Somebody's pinched a rung.
          (More struggling.)

GREEN-
HALGH   Silly bloody trick.
          (Another voice swears.)

GREEN-
HALGH   What's up?

PLIMMER I can't get my end round. Can I bust it?

GREEN-
HALGH   No. You can't bust it. If you take your end into the corner and let me get out. One good thrust and we're there.
          (Struggling is heard.)

PLIMMER Do we have to?

GREEN-
HALGH   Of course we do.

PLIMMER Why?

GREEN-
HALGH   Publicity.
          (A head emerges. It is Terry Greenhalgh, seventeen, usually saturnine. Now a bit drunk and cheerful. He is pulling the end of a huge piece of hardboard. There is a lot of puffing.)

GREEN-
HALGH   That't another thing about this firm. In case of fire you're allowed the choice of burning to death or breaking your neck on the fire escape.
          (Greenhalgh pulls; the one below pushes at the hardboard. It emerges from the hole with the inscription: 'Your Walk-Around Store' in large letters right along it. They lay it on the roof near the edge. The other boy, Gordon Plimmer, is a dimmer thing altogether.)

GREEN-
HALGH   Got the wire?

PLIMMER Yes.

(He gets a coil of wire out of his pocket and gives it to Greenhalgh. Greenhalgh is very excited, Plimmer is sick of whatever is going on. Greenhalgh pays out a length of wire and breaks it.)

GREEN-

HALGH This is the roof garden. Now you.

(Greenhalgh gives the wire to Plimmer. In both the top corners of the hardboard is a hole. Greenhalgh threads the long piece of thin wire through the hole his side. Plimmer does the same his side. Greenhalgh looks over the edge of the roof. Then he takes the unattached end of the wire and ties it to a firm part of the roof.)

GREEN-

HALGH If you spit off the edge it has an uninterrupted fall. Onto the customers. They think of everythink at Mercer's. *(He imitates a shop assistant.)* Is it raining outside, madam? *(He now imitates a customer.)* Well it was just spitting as I came in. *(He laughs.)*

(Plimmer finishes his bit of the job as if he is trapped by a madman.)

PLIMMER Finished.

(They push the hardboard right to the edge of the roof.)

GREEN-

HALGH Hold it.

PLIMMER *(doing his best)* I can't.

GREEN-

HALGH Well drop it then.

(Plimmer drops his end of the hardboard back on the roof.
Cut to a Longshot from the roof looking into the street. Z Victor Two, like a dinky toy, turns the corner and drives slowly round the block.
We cut back to Greenhalgh and Plimmer, who watch it go.)

GREEN-

HALGH Right.

PLIMMER What if somebody sees it?

GREEN-

HALGH There she goes.

(The hardboard slips some way down the front of the building and hangs crooked but very obvious.)

PLIMMER Is that it then?

GREEN-

HALGH One more little job.

PLIMMER Not another . . .

GREEN-

HALGH You wait here. This is the best.

(Plimmer waits shivery on the roof. Greenhalgh goes down the steps inside.)

Inside Mercer's Universal Stores

(*The camera looks across the shoe counter. We see that the shop is much disarrayed. Greenhalgh comes down the stairs and carefully through the shop to the door. He gets a chair, puts it down near the door and climbs up, fiddles with the burglar alarm. It goes off. That is what he wanted.*)

Back on the roof

(*Plimmer hears the alarm, cannot believe it and beats it fast.*)

Inside Mercer's Store

(*Greenhalgh knocks over the chair as he gets off it. Shoves it away and runs up the stairs.*)

On the roof

(*Plimmer is belting away. Greenhalgh follows him. The alarm bell goes on ringing.*)

The Station office

(*Blackitt is there with Taylor, who is just going off duty. The alarm is ringing.*)

BLACKITT Which one is it?

TAYLOR Eighteen.

BLACKITT I think that's Mercer's. (*Looks at list.*) Yes, Mercer's. It would be. (*Watt comes out of his office.*)

TAYLOR I'll leave it to you sarge.

WATT Trouble?

BLACKITT Mercer's. Oldham Street.

WATT Then it's trouble.

Inside Z Victor Two

(*Baker is driving. Graham talking to the girl at the information room.*)

GRAHAM Right, love. Mercer's Universal Stores. Oldham Street.

GIRL (*heard over the radio*) Message timed at zero zero five eight.

GRAHAM You're slow, love.

GIRL Correction Z Victor Two. You're fast.

The Station office

(*Blackitt and Watt are talking.*)

WATT   If anybody has to wake him, it had better be me. Bang goes my early night.

BLACKITT   He didn't do so well in the council elections, did he, old Mercer?

WATT   No. But he asked for a re-count.

BLACKITT   Fantastic.

WATT   Oh, he's a nut-case.

BLACKITT   Hear about that chap in Bolton who tried to organise some vigilantes?

WATT   No.

BLACKITT   Yes. You know. Vigilantes. To keep down hooliganism. Like Ku Klux Klan. Only shopkeepers.

WATT   No.

BLACKITT   He held a meeting but it got broken up. *(The phone rings.)* Never had any trouble like that before, or since. Newtown Police Station, Sgt Blackitt. . . . Yes.

WATT   Quick cup of tea.
(Blackitt is talking on the phone, as Watt goes towards the C.I.D. office.)

Outside Mercer's Store

(The shop window can be seen, rearranged with two models necking on a sofa. Alongside, someone has put a rough-and-ready 'X' certificate. We cut to a shot of Graham who is looking fascinated.)

Inside a phone box

(Baker is in the phone box, talking to Blackitt.)

BAKER   Yes, Sgt. That's how I'd describe it. More a work of art.

The Station office

BLACKITT   Stay there. Sergeant Watt will call for Mr Mercer. Keep your eyes skinned.
(The camera follows Blackitt as he opens the door to the C.I.D. office.)

C.I.D. office

(Watt is having a quick cup of tea. Blackitt appears in the doorway.)

WATT   Right.

Outside Mercer's shop

(Baker returns from the phone, and joins Graham, who is still fascinated by the window.)

BAKER It's a real achievement, this lot, isn't it?

GRAHAM Would you say he was round the bend, the chap who did it?

BAKER No, I'd say he was quite normal.

A converted-bus coffee bar

(*There is a crowd of youths talking and drinking, with their bikes standing by. Plimmer runs up very out of breath, and mingles with the people. He searches out Greenhalgh, and moves up to him urgently.*)

PLIMMER I thought you said you'd seen to that alarm.

GREEN-
HALGH I had.

PLIMMER Well, why did it go off then?

GREEN-
HALGH I made it.

PLIMMER (*after the briefest attempt to make sense of this*) I'm off home.

(*He gets a little way from the coffee bar, turns round and shouts.*)

PLIMMER Greenhalgh, you're barmy.

Inside Watt's car

(*Watt is driving Mr Mercer to the shop. Mercer is having occasional outbursts.*)

MERCER Is it any way to carry on? The more police you put in plain clothes, the less in uniform, right?

WATT Right.

MERCER The less in uniform, the less the criminal cares. Right?

(*Watt doesn't answer.*)

So here we are, rushing about in the middle of the night. When it's too late.

(*He slumps back in his seat.*)

If the police have given up private property, the citizen must take over.

WATT We're acting in this case, Mr Mercer.

MERCER When it's *too late*.

WATT They'll get caught.

MERCER They should have been prevented. But you can't prevent them. You're outrun, sergeant.

WATT Look, Mr Mercer. There's another side to all this you don't know about.

MERCER I know about my shop, sergeant. My neighbours know about theirs. If the police can't cope, vigilantes will.

Outside Mercer's shop

(*Watt's car draws up and stops. Mercer gets out rapidly and stops in his tracks when he sees the notice 'Your walk-around Store', dangling down in the front of the building.*)

Inside the shop

(*Mercer, Watt, Graham and Baker come in. They switch the lights on. The store sells a great variety of things. Crockery, hardwear, some clothing, shoes. Across the door are arranged three rolls of lino, two vertical and one horizontal balanced between them. As the door opens, they fall.*)

BAKER They didn't come out this way, did they?

(*Graham shuts him up.*)

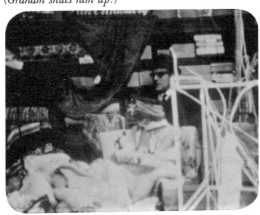

MERCER (*taking a rapid look round*) My God.

(*He sees some open drawers, goes towards them, and trips on a length of string tied knee-height across the end of the counter. He traces the string. The string from the ball on the counter has been paid out and wound round chairs, shelves, criss-crossing some areas.*)

WATT Better cut through.

MERCER Kindly don't. It's my property. If you can reclaim it, leave it.

(*In one corner an elaborate affair of clothes lines, buckets and washing bowls have been balancing together. One touch and they collapse. And as they do, a shower of drawing pins falls out of them. Plastic plates have been whizzed around the shop. Stuff has been heaped on a table with a rough notice 'Knocked Down'. In the clothing department, dummies carry beer bottles; their faces have been drawn on. Shoes have been arranged in a drunken walk round a counter.*

We see shots of the various pieces of chaos, and after each a close shot of

Mercer's horrified reaction. We follow Mercer to the hardware counter. The roughly piled goods collapse round him.)

MERCER   I wonder if you're thinking what I'm thinking?

WATT   Couldn't say.

MERCER   How much uninterrupted leisure anybody'd need to do a job like this.

(Mercer pounds up the stairs to his office, calling back.)

MERCER   Please do me the kindness of pulling down the blind.

(Watt goes up the stairs after him.)

GRAHAM   Right, sir.

WATT   Have they your permission to make a search, sir?

MERCER   Why not?

(Graham and Baker take a look at things.)

BAKER   Very interesting, psychologically, all this lot. Look at those brushes. *(He shakes his head.)* And the shape those shoes make. And the drawing pins.

GRAHAM   Drawing pins?

BAKER   I could tell you things about drawing pins that'd make your hair drop out.

A lobby upstairs, off Mercer's office

(Mercer is standing. Watt joins him.)

MERCER   There was a coat up there and some shoes in the corner.

(Watt closes the door.)

WATT   These them?

(A coat and some shoes are in a heap behind the door.)

MERCER   Oh, my God.

WATT   Why don't you sit down, Mr Mercer? Have you any way of making a cup of tea?

MERCER   Why? Do you fancy one?

WATT   Well I wouldn't say no.

MERCER   Exactly. That's the situation we're in. State servants making tea and the rest of us fending for ourselves.

WATT   I'd be glad if you'd shut up.

MERCER   Exactly.

WATT   Because I'm tired.

(Mercer goes into his office and bangs the door. Watt waits a moment and wearily goes to the door and knocks. There is no response. He opens it and looks in.)

Inside Mercer's office

(Mercer is crouched behind his desk.)

WATT   I'm sorry, sir.

(But there is no response.)

MERCER   I've heard that when a thief breaks into a house, he sometimes leaves his own filth behind. Is that so, sergeant?

WATT   It does happen, sir.

MERCER   Well I feel as if that's happened to me. Somebody's defiled my shop. He's robbed it and he despises me for letting him.

WATT   Perhaps we should go downstairs, sir, and see how far the lads have got.

MERCER   Don't try and shut me up please. This isn't just an ordinary case you can start a file on and forget it. It's a warning. Today they dare go just so far. Tomorrow they'll go further. Finally they'll show their hand and take over.

WATT   Who are 'they', sir?

MERCER   Exactly. You think it's nonsense.

WATT   Odd things do happen at two in the morning.

MERCER   The evidence is so big that nobody dare see it. Especially the police. We're infiltrated so far that it can't be long before everything collapses. Work in a shop like this and you'd see it. A well-dressed man can edge a ball of string off the counter and into his brief-case. I've seen it happen. I challenge the assistants. I say, 'Why didn't you stop him?' And they think I'm dotty. 'We didn't see a thing, Mr Mercer.' You face a brick wall. I do my best. I try and pounce. But it's beyond one man's strength.

WATT   I'd leave it to us if I were you, sir.

MERCER   What are you going to do?

WATT   Lock everything up till morning.

MERCER Will you leave a guard?

WATT What good'll that do? Whatever they wanted to do they've done.

MERCER That's it. That's just what I mean. They haven't even started!

(The camera pans with Watt out of the door.)

The lobby

WATT I'll see to the lights out here.

(He goes and turns off the light in the lobby.)

MERCER *(calling from the office)* Sergeant.

WATT Yes?

Back in Mercer's office

(Watt comes into the office. Mercer turns off the desk light.)

MERCER Look down there. *(He nods towards the window. Watt looks out. We see him and Mercer from outside the venetian blind.)*

(Cut to the pavement beneath, where pausing for a moment is Greenhalgh. He turns and walks off.)

(Again we see Mercer and Watt through the venetion blind.)

Inside Mercer's office

WATT Do you know him?

MERCER His name's Greenhalgh.

WATT Well?

MERCER He works here.

WATT Do you think he could help us?

MERCER Yes.

WATT Right. (*He goes out of the room and shouts down the stairs.*) Baker! Get in the car and pick up a lad about eighteen. Dark hair. Wearing a mac. Up the street Woolworth's direction. Might have got as far as the lights.

Below in the shop

(*We see Baker and Graham getting the message.*)
BAKER Right, sergeant.
(*Baker belts out of the shop.*)

The street outside

(*Z Victor Two is still outside shop. Baker dashes out, takes a quick look up road, gets into the car and is off. As the car goes, the camera holds the shop front.*)

Inside the shop

(*Greenhalgh is sitting in a chair. Watt is talking to him. Mercer is watching some way off. The police are standing by.*)

GREEN-
HALGH I was on my way home.
WATT Where do you live?
GREEN-
HALGH New Street.
WATT Do they know you're out?
GREEN-
HALGH I expect so.

WATT	Why are you so late going home?
GREEN-HALGH	Been out.
WATT	Where've you been?
GREEN-HALGH	Look. Do I have to explain everything? I was only passing the door.
WATT	You were loitering. Where've you been?
GREEN-HALGH	Had a few drinks.
WATT	You're under age, aren't you?
GREEN-HALGH	You asked me where I'd been. I've had a few drinks.
WATT	By yourself?
GREEN-HALGH	Some of the time.
WATT	Who were you with the rest of it?
GREEN-HALGH	Friends.
WATT	Who?
GREEN-HALGH	A friend.
WATT	What's his name?
GREEN-HALGH	Do I have to give names?
WATT	Nobody's accusing you of anything, lad. I'm asking questions. If you know the answers, you'd better tell me who were you with?
GREEN-HALGH	Gordon Plimmer.
WATT	Gordon Plimmer. Well that's all I asked you. We want you to help us, that's all. Nobody's forcing you. What does he do, Gordon Plimmer?
GREEN-HALGH	Heaversedge's Garage.
WATT	Heaversedge's Garage. (*Looking at him*) What were you doing outside?
GREEN-HALGH	Passing.
WATT	You'd stopped.
GREEN-HALGH	(*in close-up*) Having a look.
WATT	Interested?

GREEN-HALGH	Yes.
WATT	Why didn't you come in?
	(*Greenhalgh cannot answer.*)
	The natural thing would be to come in. You work here, don't you?
GREENHALGH	Yes.
WATT	So why didn't you come in?
GREEN-HALGH	The police were here already.
WATT	Wouldn't have made any difference. We don't bite.
	(*There is a pause.*)
	What number New Street did you say?
GREEN-HALGH	Eighteen.
WATT	Eighteen. Right, lad. That's all. Good night.
GREEN-HALGH	Thanks.
WATT	No. We thank you.
	(*Greenhalgh gets up. The camera follows him, to show Mercer in the background. He is very surprised.*)
MERCER	Do you know who it is then?
WATT	No. Do you?
MERCER	Of course I do. It's him.
WATT	Mr Mercer. You can't make guesses. You've got to know.
MERCER	I know all about him. He's got a record.
WATT	Hold on a minute, lad.
MERCER	I only took him on because I was asked to. He's got a record as long as your arm. The Probation Officer rang me up. He said you've got a lad applying for a job. Well, give him one and I'll vouch for him. Don't let on. Just treat him like anybody else. So I did. That was my effort at public service. Well, I've learned a thing or two about public service since then and I shan't make the same mistake twice.
WATT	You'd better stop there, sir.
MERCER	I shan't stop there. I've had enough cat and mouse. He knows the shop. He knows the area. This lot happens and he's alongside. It'd look damned suspicious if he were a raving salvationist. But he's not. He's the criminal type.
WATT	Better beat it lad.
	(*Greenhalgh moves off at high speed.*)
	You pull yourself together and get off home, Sir.
MERCER	I'm stopping here.

WATT (*to Baker and Graham*) Check the doors and windows. These lads can take you home in the car.
(*Watt goes to Mercer who's crouched on a chair.*)
Luckily for you, I choose to overlook that outburst, Mr Mercer.
MERCER If you do, you'll regret it.

Outside Mercer's shop

(*Mercer and the police come out and get into the cars. The streets are quite deserted. Just before the scene fades we cut to a shot of Terry Greenhalgh, waiting in a nearby alleyway.*)

The interior of the C.I.D. office the next morning

(*Barlow is hanging his coat up with one eye on various papers propped up near him. The camera pans with him as he moves through into the outer office.*)

The Station office

(*Blackitt is just getting his coat on.*)
BARLOW When's this timed?
BLACKITT That's two ten this morning, sir. Break-in. Rearrangement of stuff. More like a practical joke.
BARLOW And this is half an hour ago.
BLACKITT Eight twenty. When Mr Mercer got to the shop. Just phoned in.
BARLOW Well, they don't tally do they?
BLACKITT No. They don't, sir.
BARLOW It would be Mercer.
BLACKITT Yes, sir.
BARLOW Just off Blackie?
BLACKITT That's it, sir.
BARLOW Spare us five minutes, will you, Blackie?
BLACKIE Yes sir . . . Sgt Watt . . .
BARLOW Why not, he started it. He may as well carry on and sort it out.
(*Barlow returns to his office. Blackitt picks up the telephone.*)

Inside Mercer's shop

(*The shop is shut. A close shot of woman mopping-up water on floor. Outside the window shoppers and passers-by are looking in. Inside the assistants are standing by their counters. The senior assistant is taking Watt round.*)

SENIOR
ASSISTANT Everything's exactly as we found it, sergeant. Well *I* found it, as a matter of fact and got straight onto Mr Mercer. These walls are only hardboard, you see and the water came straight through. This stuff's a wash-out (*indicating shelves*).

WATT Could it have been an accident?

SENIOR
ASSISTANT Not from yesterday. You were here during the night, sergeant and the tap wasn't running then, was it? . . . Besides, the plug was in. And these shelves have been cleared.
(*We see a close shot of plates and cups and sugar bowls on the floor.*)

SENIOR
ASSISTANT The front door was wide open when I arrived, with a notice on it.

WATT What did it say?

SENIOR
ASSISTANT 'The best things in life are free.' And he's danced on the broom handles. They're all smashed. We haven't touched a thing.

WATT Is that all? (*He doesn't share the assistant's enthusiasm.*)

SENIOR
ASSISTANT That's all. Would you like to see Mr Mercer?

WATT All right.

SENIOR
ASSISTANT He's up there.
(*Watt goes upstairs. The assistants still stand by their counters, enjoying the break in routine.*)

Inside Mercer's office

(*Mercer is sitting vacantly behind his desk. Watt comes in, trying to break the air of doom around Mercer.*)

WATT   I've seen round, thanks, Mr Mercer. Nothing to stop you clearing up a bit. We'll need to know if there's anything missing. So that we'll know what the charge is.

MERCER   Greenhalgh cleared out his locker, sergeant.

WATT   I've got a note of it. Thanks.

MERCER   And are you satisfied?

WATT   If you mean 'am I pleased?', of course I'm not.

Downstairs in the shop

(*The senior assistant is talking to a press photographer.*)

SENIOR ASSISTANT   No. Just as it is now. We haven't moved a thing.

(*The photographer takes a snap. Watt comes down the stairs.*)

WATT   Have you got a phone?

SENIOR ASSISTANT   Out the back, sergeant.

WATT   Try one of the windows. The *Evening Post* likes it hot.

(*He goes to the phone.*)

PHOTO-GRAPHER   What about now?

SENIOR ASSISTANT   You could try.

PHOTO-GRAPHER   Where is he?

SENIOR ASSISTANT   Upstairs.

(*The photographer goes upstairs.*)

Back in the Station office

(*Police Constable Taylor picks up the phone.*)

TAYLOR   Newtown . . . Yes, sergeant. Mercer's.

The Shop

(*Watt is on the phone.*)

WATT   I want to talk to Terry Greenhalgh, eighteen, New Street. Got that? Graham and Baker have seen him. So they'd better pick him up. I've got one call to make. Heaversedge's Garage, then I'll be back.

The Station office

TAYLOR Right, sergeant. I'll get things moving.

The work area in Heaversedge's garage

(Gordon Plimmer is cleaning a car. In the distance, he sees Watt come into the garage, look round, talk to a mechanic and get directed into the Boss's office. When the coast is clear Plimmer beats it. We hear the sound of a door slamming and a bolt going over. Watt and Mr Heaversedge come out of the office into the work area. They look around and move purposefully and together out of the camera's shot.)

Another part of the garage

(We see a close shot of a door marked 'Men'. The camera pulls back to show Watt and Heaversedge standing beside it. Heaversedge is knocking at the door and listening.)

HEAVERS-
   EDGE Gordon . . . Gordon . . . He only wants to ask a few questions . . . Gordon. If you don't come out I shall get annoyed . . . Gordon . . . The longer you stay in there the more you'll have to explain away.

WATT It looks worse every minute, lad. Come on out.
(The sound of a chain being pulled is heard. The bolt is drawn back. Out comes Plimmer.)

PLIMMER Can I wash me hands?

HEAVERS-
   EDGE In a minute.
(Plimmer stands still.)

WATT Now. Terry Greenhalgh. He's a friend of yours.
(There is no reply.)

84

WATT And you were with him last night?

PLIMMER No.

WATT He says you were.

PLIMMER He would. He's barmy.

(*Watt opens his notebook.*)

WATT Right. Now. About Mercer's. Tell me if I'm wrong. Broke in. Smashed crockery, broke kitchen utensils, left tap running in cloakroom, pounds worth of damage by water, front door left open. Theft of goods.

(*We see a close shot of Plimmer's amazed reaction.*)

Anything to add before I take you off?

PLIMMER We didn't do any of that.

WATT I thought you weren't there.

PLIMMER It's not us.

WATT Want to come and have a look?

PLIMMER You're after somebody else.

WATT Why didn't you come out of there and tell me then? You could have saved me a lot of time.

PLIMMER I didn't know what you wanted.

WATT But you'd got something to hide, hadn't you? Eh? Mercer's between eleven and one. You and Terry Greenhalgh. And when you saw me out there you locked yourself in the lavatory.

PLIMMER We didn't do all that lot.

WATT What did you do then?

PLIMMER We had, more like, a laugh.

(*Cut to medium shot of street door from inside.*)

Door of eighteen New Street

(*We see the shadows of Graham and Baker through the glass of the door.*)

GRAHAM Try again.

(*Baker knocks again. Nothing happens. The camera tracks in on the Letter Box, and we see Graham's eyes through it.*)

VOICE I'm here.

Outside the house door

(*Baker and Graham turn round. Mrs Greenhalgh enters the shot.*)

GRAHAM Mrs Greenhalgh?

MRS GREEN-
HALGH Yes.

GRAHAM We couldn't get a reply.

MRS GREEN-	
HALGH	No. You wouldn't.
BAKER	Could we come in a minute?
GRAHAM	I'll hold those.
	(*He takes her shopping bags. She looks for her key in her purse and unlocks the door.*)
MRS GREEN-	
HALGH	Keep your voices down.
	(*They go inside quietly.*)

Inside the hall

MRS GREEN-	
HALGH	(*whispering*) I'll have them. Thanks.
GRAHAM	Where do you want them put?
MRS GREEN-	
HALGH	I can manage.
	(*She goes off with the shopping bags into the kitchen.*)
MR GREEN-	
HALGH	(*in kitchen*) It came open.
MRS GREEN-	
HALGH	(*in kitchen*) You could have shut it.
	(*The sound of a stove door being shut. Mrs Greenhalgh comes out of the kitchen, indicates the front room and goes in. They follow her. She shuts the door. From the kitchen comes the sound of a slow chesty cough.*)

The front room

MRS GREEN-	
HALGH	Now you can tell me. I didn't want his dad to hear. What's he done?
BAKER	Your Terry's not at work this morning and we'd like to ask him a few questions. Is he in?
MRS GREEN-	
HALGH	Eh?
BAKER	Could we have a word with your Terry, I wonder.
MRS GREEN-	
HALGH	Do you know where he is?
BAKER	No. Do you?
MRS GREEN	
HALGH	Could be anywhere.
MR GREEN-	
HALGH	(*from kitchen*) Olive.

MRS GREEN-
HALGH Yes.
VOICE It's open again.
MRS GREEN-
HALGH I'm coming. (*To the police*) Excuse me. (*She leaves the room.*)
(*Graham and Baker have a chance to see the room. There is a plaque on the wall. A large eye with an inscription 'God the unseen guest'.*)
MR GREEN-
HALGH (*in kitchen*) You put too much on at once.
MRS GREEN-
HALGH (*in kitchen*) I don't want it to go out.
BAKER (*to Graham*) You have a go.
(*Mrs Greenhalgh comes back.*)
GRAHAM Mrs Greenhalgh. You didn't look a bit surprised when you saw us. You might have been expecting us.
MRS GREEN-
HALGH I was.

GRAHAM What for? . . . What's the matter?
MRS GREEN-
HALGH I'm at my band's end I can tell you. I've made such an effort and I find I can't sleep.
GRAHAM What have you tried to do?
MRS GREEN-
HALGH Warn him. After all he's my son, isn't he? Make him wake up to the danger. Show him where he's going.
GRAHAM What do you . . .

MRS GREEN-HALGH	But it has no effect. I may as well shut up for all the notice he takes. He's hardened.

GRAHAM What do you mean?

MRS GREEN-HALGH The life he lives and the friends he's got. He thinks I don't notice. But I do. Every word. About somewhere he's been or somebody he's friendly with. And things, things in his pockets. He's living the sort of life his dad and I would be ashamed of and he's dragging us down with him. We had a go at him yesterday. That's why I asked you to keep quiet. His dad's still upset. And he swore at us. If his dad had been a fit man, he'd have killed him.

GRAHAM What did you say to him to make him do that?

MRS GREEN-HALGH His dad and me tried to make him see what he was doing to us. His dad doesn't talk to him very often and he did go a bit far, but he's a sick man at the end of his tether. So you can excuse him a bit. But not Terry. Right in the middle of it. While his dad was still talking. He swore. Our Terry. Standing in that kitchen. Well, he never heard that sort of thing from us. And he left the house. I couldn't move a muscle. His dad was going to follow him but he's not fit. But when he'd gone I thought to myself. Thank God I thought. He's had an upright home. He's been told what's what. He's been shown the way. And he's rejected it. So he can fend for himself. It's a load off my mind.

GRAHAM Where is he?

MRS GREEN-HALGH If you want to find out Terry, go to the bars and the billiard places and them low cafes. Where you'd expect that type. But don't imagine *we* can help you. Because we can't.

BAKER Has he been in trouble with the police before, Mrs Greenhalgh?

MRS GREEN-HALGH Yes he has. He's done a year on probation.

BAKER When was that?

MRS GREEN-HALGH Three years ago. I thought we were hard on him then but his dad was right, I was wrong. You can't see it at the time.

GRAHAM What did he do?

MRS GREEN-HALGH He took some money.

GRAHAM Where from?

S GREEN-
HALGH   One holiday week. All his pals were going to Blackpool and places. So he took his fare out of his dad's pocket. And the rest out of my purse. He said he was going to put it back but his dad didn't give him the chance. He took him to court. His dad was always very straight. And he got a year's probation. I prayed it would stop there. But it didn't. I don't know what they do with them on probation but if you ask me—that was the start.

R GREEN-
HALGH   *(from kitchen)* Olive.

S GREEN-
HALGH   Yes.

GRAHAM   Thanks Mrs Greenhalgh. *(To Baker)* Come on. *(To Mrs Greenhalgh)* We'll let you know what happens.

R GREEN-
HALGH   Olive.

S GREEN-
HALGH   Don't make a noise.
   (They go out into the hall.)

The hall

(Mrs Greenhalgh opens the front door and lets Graham and Baker out.)

GREEN-
HALGH   *(from kitchen)* Who is it, Olive?

GREEN-
HALGH   Nobody.

The C.I.D. office

(Barlow and Watt are looking at the local newspaper.)

BARLOW   We could have done without the photograph.

WATT   We could have done without the statement from Mercer.

BARLOW   That photograph's the thing though. The written bits can get overlooked.
   (The telephone rings and Barlow picks it up.) Yes. *(Hands telephone to Watt.)*

WATT   *(on phone)* Not at all.

Inside a phone box

BAKER   She doesn't know where he is Sarge. One thing, he's done a year on probation. She's got a pretty low opinion of him. Bars and billiard halls. *(He listens)* Yes, Sarge, we'll do the rounds.

The C.I.D. office

WATT And, quick, which probation officer, did she say?

The phone box

BAKER She didn't. It's a very funny set up, this family, sarge.

The C.I.D. office

(*Barlow slams the newspaper down.*)

WATT (*still on phone*) Tell me later. When you've found him.

(*He rings off. Barlow points to something in the paper.*)

WATT (*without looking*) The last bit?

(*Barlow nods.*)

BARLOW Do you think we're inadequate and overworked, John?

WATT Not all the time.

BARLOW That's the spirit. Let's get it cleared up before the late edition, eh?

(*Barlow drops the paper into the waste paper basket. Watt goes out into main office.*)

The Station office

WATT (*speaking to Taylor at the counter*) If Graham and Baker have anything to say, I'm round at the Probation Office.

The C.I.D. office

(*Barlow crumples the newspaper and throws it into the waste paper basket.*)

Inside Z Victor Two

(*Baker and Graham are driving in silence.*)

BAKER There's a little dive just off here. We could try that.

GRAHAM We could. (*There's a silence.*) There's nothing worse than religion when it gets bent.

The Probation Office corridor

(*Watt enters the corridor and knocks on the door. We see a close shot of the label on the door: 'Mr K. Aspin'.*)

ASPIN Come in.

Inside Aspin's office

(*The probation officer is talking to a boy. When he sees Watt coming in Aspin gets up fast taking Watt out of the office and shutting the door behind him.*)

The corridor

WATT Sorry. I thought you might be by yourself this time of day.

ASPIN You know what it's like. What's up?

WATT A lad, Terry Greenhalgh. Works at Mercer's. Was he one of yours?

ASPIN Yes. Why?

WATT Trouble.

ASPIN Give me five minutes?

WATT O.K.

(*Watt sits on a bench in the corridor.*)

ASPIN Could you wait round there? (*He points down the corridor.*) Where you can't upset the customers.

WATT As you like.

ASPIN Nothing personal.

(*Aspin goes back into his office in a good humour. Watt sits on another bench the other side of a partition where anyone coming from a Probation Office can't see him.*)

An amusement arcade

(*We see the reflection of Graham in a distorting mirror. The camera pulls back showing Graham through the youths who are crossing the foreground. He looks around arcade. Nobody seems worried. He goes.*)

The Probation Office corridor

(*Watt is behind the partition. There is the sound of door opening and voices.*)

ASPIN No thanks. It's more serious than that. I had to leave it at the garage. Thanks though.

BOY I mended me Uncle Alfred's.

ASPIN Next time you can have a go at mine.

BOY Can I?

ASPIN See you next week.

BOY Ta ra.

(The outer door slams. Aspin appears round the partition.)

ASPIN You can come out now.

WATT Well, thanks. I like to feel wanted.

ASPIN No, it's that particular lad. Once he gets the idea I have a friend in the police, I may as well give up.

WATT He must be disturbed.

(They go into the office.)

Inside Aspin's office

ASPIN Sit down. Now then, What's up?

WATT Have you read the *Evening Post*?

ASPIN Can't afford it.

WATT Well, take mine. Read that bit and then I'll fill it in for you.

(Watt hands over the paper.)

Z Victor Two

(Graham climbs in.)

BAKER That didn't take long.

GRAHAM I didn't dawdle. No joy. Try one more? Molloy's eh?

(Baker starts the engine.)

(We see Z Victor Two move off. There is some slight irregularity in the driving.)

GRAHAM No wonder you took so long to pass your advanced driving.

BAKER My driving *was* advanced. It was my English I failed on.

GRAHAM Get away.

BAKER I did. They don't appreciate style. I made him feel inadequate.

GRAHAM Aye. There was a chap called Evans in Bradford. And he was more like a poet. You know. Lyrical. Well on his test the examiner told him to describe the road as he went along. So he turned a corner and said: 'Now we are going into a twisty-twindy lane.' And do you know what the examiner said?

BAKER No.

GRAHAM He said 'Welcome to Bleeding Fairy land' Quick as a flash.

BAKER And he failed?

GRAHAM No. He passed.

Inside Aspin's office

ASPIN It's not what you'd call a pure crime, is it?

WATT Damage to property is a crime.

ASPIN I know, but there's a context. Isn't there? The first go was a sort of demonstration, wasn't it?

WATT That's a way of putting it.

ASPIN And the second was more a retaliation. . . . You can't separate what Greenhalgh did from the things Mercer said to him. . . . And then there's the whole family setting as well. You can't just pick out the criminal bits and forget the rest.

WATT But you think he did it?

ASPIN Sounds like it.

WATT Where d'you think he'd be?

ASPIN Where have you looked?

WATT He's not at work. Of course. He's not at home. The lads got an idea of some likely spots from his mother. They're following them up.

ASPIN Well I can tell you one thing. He's not in any of them. Oh my God. It's complicated. She thinks he's damned. He thinks she's crackers. But she's his mother so he still depends on her. But she can't stand the weight. So he, being a malicious little swine as well, drops names and places and clues about his life of crime. To see how far she'll go believing him. And she goes all the way. She thinks he's a Newtown Al Capone. She's scared of her own imagination. And in the meantime, he works at Mercer's.

WATT   Is his father dead?

ASPIN   They haven't got a certificate for him. But he sits in the kitchen with hotwater bottles tucked round him and looks at the fire. When all those houses went smokeless, they had to change the open fire for a coke stove. But he didn't move.

WATT   It's a mess isn't it?

ASPIN   If it didn't involve people's lives it would be funny.

WATT   You seem to keep up with him.

ASPIN   On and off. It's two years since his probation finished. But I make a point of saying hello.

WATT   He didn't sleep at home last night evidently.

ASPIN   Have you tried his grandmother?

WATT   His mother didn't mention that.

ASPIN   No. She wouldn't. They don't speak. What time is it?

WATT   (*looks at watch*) Crikey. Half twelve.

ASPIN   If he's sticking to his routine, he'll be having a swim.

WATT   Where?

ASPIN   Blucher Street baths. I have one meself on Thursdays. That's where we meet sometimes, I'd have one today but the car's bust.

WATT   Like me to drive you round? If you don't want to break your routine.

ASPIN   Well . . . I do keep me things here . . .

WATT   If it makes it any easier, I'll wear a beard.

ASPIN   Right. A swim and a sandwich and back for half one.

The grubby entrance to Molloy's cafe

(*Z Victor Two draws up. Graham gets out of the car and goes down the steps.*)

Inside Molloy's cafe

(*Graham walks in and looks round. Everybody watches him.*)

GRAHAM   Anything out the back?

MOLLOY   If you can't wait you're welcome.
        (*There is a laugh from the regulars.*)

GRAHAM   No thanks. (*He goes to the counter.*) Name Greenhalgh mean anything to you?

MOLLOY   We've had a Sam, but he moved on.

GRAHAM   His name's Terry, and he's no' but a lad.

MOLLOY   No. Not me. Hey, Matt, does the name Terry Greenhalgh mean anything to you?

GRAHAM   (*correcting his pronounciation*) Greenhalgh—halgh—halgh.

Inside Z Victor Two

BAKER *(talking to B.D.)* We're trying the dives but nobody seems to have heard of him . . . By the railway station. This is the last call . . . Then we'll be back.

B.D. Thank you, Z Victor Two.

(Baker puts down the phone and notices something odd going on in the street.)

The Street outside

(We are looking out of Z Victor Two window. An old man and a young man are seen coming over the crossing. The old man is clinging to the young man or vice versa. The young man called Sampson is a university student and wears a scarf. The old man, Carroll, is Irish and looks pretty seedy. They approach the car.)

Inside Z Victor Two

(Carroll and Sampson reach the window of the car.)

SAMPSON *(looking pretty unhappy)* Excuse me, constable.

BAKER Yes?

SAMPSON Er . . . if you're not too busy, I have a problem . . .

CARROLL He has that, sir.

BAKER All right. I'm listening.

SAMPSON Well, it's a bit difficult now I come to say it . . .

CARROLL It's quite true, sir. Every word. I've put him in an unenviable position, sir, with me anti-social habits.

BAKER You're what?

CARROLL I can't break meself, sir. It's right, sir, what he says.

BAKER He hasn't said anything yet.

CARROLL You'd better tell him, sir, and get it over. I won't deny it. (*Nudging Sampson*) Go on, sir.

SAMPSON I'm not sure I want to.

CARROLL You're too good, sir. Let me. I took his case. Didn't I, sir? I took your case. Right where it was standing. I can't bear to see you suffer . . . Now you know . . . And I feel better for getting it out of my system.

(Carroll is very moved. Baker turns to Sampson.)

BAKER In your own words, please, sir . . .

CARROLL Yes. It'll come better from you. Scarf and all.

(Sampson is finding a way out now.)

BAKER Well, go on . . .

SAMPSON Well, I was in the station arcade and I wanted to get an evening paper so I left my case in the alley way and went to get one. I was back two minutes later and this man had picked up my case and was away.

CARROLL If I'd a decent pair of shoes, nobody would have caught me. With all due respect, sir.

SAMPSON So I . . . ran after him.

CARROLL He collared me, sir, and it was a fair cop.

BAKER *(looking at Sampson)* What are you looking so miserable for?

SAMPSON Well I don't like making trouble and I've got my case back.

BAKER What about all the other cases lying about all over the station? What's going to happen to them?

CARROLL *(woebegone)* Exactly, sir.

SAMPSON *(after thinking for a moment)* I suppose so.

(*There is another pause.*)
Well that's it, then. He took my case.
(*Again he pauses.*)
Do I leave a name and address?

BAKER You hop in the back please, sir. (*To Carroll*) And you too.

SAMPSON Do I have to?

BAKER It'd be a public service if you did, sir.

SAMPSON (*after another small think during which time Carroll doesn't dare to look at him*) Oh, well. That's that then. Isn't it?
(*Opens the door and signalling to Carroll. Carroll gets in smartly.*)

BAKER (*to Sampson*) Have you got a train to catch?

SAMPSON 5.30.

BAKER You'll make it.
(*Sampson gets in. As they settle, Graham comes back.*)

GRAHAM What the heck . . . ?

BAKER Taking 'em in.

GRAHAM You're not one for wasting time, are you?

BAKER What about you then?

GRAHAM Drew a blank. Of course.

BAKER Oh, Bad luck.
(*Baker starts the engine.*)

Inside the Baths

(*A close shot of Greenhalgh swimming. Zoom back to a long shot from the gallery. We see that others are swimming too.*)

The observer's gallery in the Baths

(*Watt and Aspin are looking down*)

ASPIN You see. It's easy when you know where to look.

WATT Hm.

ASPIN I suppose you'll take him in straight off.

WATT It's what I came for.

ASPIN (*sarcastically*) He'll like that.

WATT How do you mean?

ASPIN Well, they get at him at home. Mercer has a go at work. He only needs to know the police are onto him as well and it'll isolate him completely. And if he's going to go wrong that's the first thing he wants. Isolation.

WATT For God's sake, man. Don't be wet. He's wrecked a shop. I'm all for advances in education, but this takes free expression too far. He's got to answer for it.

ASPIN I brought you here didn't I?

WATT Yes.

ASPIN You wouldn't have known if I'd not told you?

WATT No.

ASPIN Well then. You go back to the station. I'll talk to Greenhalgh and try and get him to come to you voluntarily. If he won't you come and get him. But I think he just might. He's not stupid and I think he trusts me. If I can get him to separate in his mind the damage he's done from the reason he's done it, I might get him to take the blame. And that would be a step forward, wouldn't it? He could start coping with the other things after that. He just might, eh?

WATT Hm.

ASPIN This one case.

WATT It's unusual procedure, you know.

ASPIN It's an unusual case.

WATT They all are. What if I said no?

ASPIN You'd be quite within your rights.
(Watt feels very uncomfortable, and thinks.)

WATT No hanging about?

ASPIN No.

WATT I want me head seeing to . . . O.K. . . . This once . . . But the end's the same. We get him.

ASPIN You'll get him. But no cars, no cops, no pushing.

WATT You see, it would be different if I were a free agent. But I'm not. I work for a boss.

Inside the C.I.D. office

(Barlow is interviewing Sampson and Carroll, with Baker standing by.)

BARLOW You left your case, did you?

SAMPSON Yes.

BARLOW And you took it?

CARROLL Afraid so, sir. It's a habit I'm trying to break meself of.

BARLOW And you saw it happen?

BAKER No, sir. It had happened when it came to my notice.

BARLOW So you reported it?

SAMPSON Yes.

BARLOW And you accept what he says?

CARROLL I do, sir. With shame.
(For a long time Barlow looks from one to the other. Sampson looks agonised. Carroll looks relieved after his confession.)

BARLOW But I don't see it. You're just not that kind of man.

CARROLL What kind would that be, sir?

BARLOW You're not the kind to do a thing like that. You don't creep about railway stations looking for stray cases.

CARROLL At one time, no, sir. But now . . .

BARLOW You don't give yourself credit, Mr Carroll. You'd never do a thing like that.

CARROLL It's a credit to your generosity, sir. But I did.

BARLOW Never.

CARROLL I did.

BARLOW I don't believe you.

CARROLL I took his case.

BARLOW Nonsense.

CARROLL Sir.

BARLOW Nonsense.

CARROLL Sir.

BARLOW It doesn't hold water. You were nowhere near his case. You didn't even know his case existed. You've been wrongly accused. It's a pack of lies. I know your type, Mr Carroll and I'm on your side. You're innocent.

CARROLL I'm not. I'm not, sir. Ask him.

BARLOW He's lying.

(Sampson is looking very uncomfortable.)

CARROLL He's not, sir.

BARLOW You never stole his case.

CARROLL I did. Of course I did.

BARLOW Liar.

(Barlow is working Carroll into an agitated state while Sampson looks shiftier. Carroll bursts out.)

CARROLL I haven't come here to be accused of lying. I took his case. I took it while he went to buy a paper. You can ask him if I didn't and he'll have to say yes, because he let me do it.

(He freezes, as he realises what he has admitted. We see a close shot of Barlow.)

BARLOW He let you do it?

CARROLL He let me do it and I am not a liar.

BARLOW Beat it, Mr Carroll . . . Go on, get out, off. *(Sampson rises too.)* Not you. *(Sampson sits down again.)* Nor you. *(To Baker who was about to leave.)*

(Carroll leaves. Barlow is left with Baker and Sampson.)

SAMPSON He wanted to get to prison, you see inspector.

BARLOW I know that. *(To Baker)* Did you?

BAKER No, sir.

BARLOW No. *(To Sampson)* You're a very silly man, Mr Sampson, and you've wasted valuable police time.

SAMPSON I'm sorry sir.

BARLOW As if it wasn't hard enough without jokes. You're a student aren't you, Mr Sampson?

SAMPSON Yes, sir.

BARLOW And what are you studying?

SAMPSON Psychology, sir.

BARLOW Psychology, hear that, Baker?

BAKER Yes, sir.

BARLOW Psychology. (*To Sampson*) A word in your ear, Mr Sampson, lad. Don't you bring the patients to us. Let us bring them to you, eh?

Inside the Station office

(*Watt comes in and looks round as if he's pinched something.*)

WATT Graham and Baker?

TAYLOR Baker with Inspector Barlow, sarge. Graham having a cup of tea.

WATT Having a cup of tea, is he?

TAYLOR He was asking for you, sergeant.

WATT Oh, having a cup of tea, is he?

TAYLOR Graham? (*Watt nods.*) Yes, sergeant.

(*Watt is about to do the same when the c.i.d. door opens and Sampson and Baker come out. Sampson tries a conciliatory smile to Baker, but gets nothing back. Watt tries to make himself scarce without being obvious about it. But . . .*)

BARLOW'S
VOICE That you, John?

WATT Yes, sir.

(*He goes into the office.*)

The C.I.D. Office

BARLOW There's a pile of stuff waiting for you.
(*Watt immediately takes an unusually deep interest in the new stuff.*)
Well?

WATT All buttoned up, sir. Greenhalgh. You needn't worry.

BARLOW Good, Graham and Baker drew a blank on the underworld.

WATT You can forget about it, sir. He'll be here very shortly.
(*Watt returns to his papers. Barlow doesn't take his eyes off him.*)
Did we get Thompson's jacket back from the labs, sir?

BARLOW Yes, John. The glass dust on it is the same as the back window of the Essoldo.

WATT So that's all right. Did Smith and Weir search the garage at four, Hebden Street?

BARLOW Report's under your nose.

WATT Oh yes. I'll get down to it straight away. It's not worth taking the rest of my day off.
(*Watt tries to go. Barlow slams his desk.*)

BARLOW What's got into everybody, John?

WATT Sir?

BARLOW 'Greenhalgh'll be here shortly?' Why isn't he here now?

WATT Ah, well . . .

BARLOW Shut the door, come back and sit down.
(*Watt does as he is told.*)
Now then. Explain.

WATT I struck a bargain sir. It was the only way I could get what I wanted. But it'll be all the same in the end.

BARLOW All right. Sounds reasonable. Only tell me.

WATT Yes, sir.
(*As he starts to, we cut to:*)

Inside the Baths

(*The probation officer is ready to dive. He does so and starts swimming. Greenhalgh sees him and nonchalantly climbs out of the bath and goes under a shower.*
Aspin, having swum to the other end, looks around for Greenhalgh. Can't see him. He swims to the side and holds the pipes. Greenhalgh has come out of the shower and is rubbing his hair with his towel. Aspin climbs out of the bath.
Greenhalgh, passing, stops when he hears Aspin.)

ASPIN How do?
(*Aspin joins Greenhalgh.*)

GREEN-
HALGH Hello.

   (*He makes to go. Aspin shouts after him.*)

ASPIN Hey. Come and sit down here. I want to talk to you. Come on.

   (*They sit on the side of the bath.*)

   They tell me you found out I'd got you your job at Mercer's.

GREEN-
HALGH Who told you that?

ASPIN Oh. It gets around. Anyway, you don't mind, else you wouldn't talk to me, would you?

GREEN-
HALGH I don't mind.

ASPIN How's your Mum and Dad?

GREEN-
HALGH No change.

ASPIN Where did you sleep last night?

GREEN-
HALGH At me grandma's. Anything wrong with that?

ASPIN No, you can sleep where you like for all I care.

   (*Aspin leaves Greenhalgh, and swims off the width of the bath and back.*

   Greenhalgh just sits. Aspin stops again by him.)

ASPIN You still here?

   (*There is the sound of Aspin leaving the water.*)

GREEN-
HALGH Did they send you?

   (*Aspin joins Greenhalgh.*)

ASPIN Who? The cops? Old Mercer? Or your Mum?

GREEN-
HALGH   Any of 'em.

ASPIN   None of 'em. I came for a swim.

GREEN-
HALGH   But you know don't you?

ASPIN   Of course I know. So do the police. So does old Mercer. And so
does your Mum. And it's only a matter of time before they make
you pay for it.

GREEN-
HALGH   What about them? Why can't they get off my back?

ASPIN   I'm not talking about them. I'm talking about you.

GREEN-
HALGH   You're one of 'em yourself.

ASPIN   If you say that again, I'll belt you one. I'm not one of anybody. I'm
me. If you like, only if you like, mind, I'll tell you the best thing to
do, shall I? You're number one suspect. There's a photo in the
paper.

GREEN-
HALGH   Is there?

ASPIN   Not you. Just the shop. But the police are after *you*.

GREEN-
HALGH   Did they tell you?

ASPIN   I was approached. Because I knew you. They were onto me
straight away.

GREEN-
HALGH   They don't forget, do they?

ASPIN   You've got to understand the police mind. It's a study in itself.
Are you interested?
(*Greenhalgh nods.*)

ASPIN   Right. Give me time for a swim round and I'll come out and
tell you what I'd do in your shoes. Only if you want me to,
mind. It's up to you. Otherwise, see you.

GREEN-
HALGH   I'll be getting me pants on.
(*He watches, then moves away.*)

Inside C.I.D. office

(*A close shot of Barlow talking to Watt.*)

BARLOW   Correct me if I'm wrong. A shop was broken into. Damage
estimated at four hundred pounds. The owner spoke to the press
and the press published remarks critical of the police. Those crit-
icisms can only be answered one way and that's by finding the

103

person responsible and charging him. Would you say that was a fair summary?

WATT Yes, sir.

BARLOW You accept those priorities, do you, because if you don't we aren't on common ground any more.

WATT He's going to be charged, sir.

BARLOW When?

WATT As soon as he walks through that door.

BARLOW In his own good time. You've been talking to somebody, John or reading Penguin books on psychology. You're not yourself. I'll help you out. Graham and Baker know this Greenhalgh. That right?

WATT Yes, sir.

BARLOW Get 'em down to Blucher Street Baths and bring Greenhalgh back here regardless of his preferences.

WATT Sir . . .

BARLOW (*in a close shot*) Now.

WATT Yes, sir.

(*He goes to do it.*)

The observation gallery at the Baths

(*We hear the noise of people swimming below. Aspin and Greenhalgh are sitting in the balcony and looking down.*)

GREEN-
HALGH Old Mercer's not been the same since he got chucked off the Council. And he had to take it out on somebody. He's a bit bent if you ask me.

ASPIN Why pick on you?

GREEN-
HALGH Don't know.

ASPIN Come on. You must have fooled about.

GREEN-
HALGH No worse than the others. And not as much after he warned me.

ASPIN When was that?

GREEN-
HALGH Last week. He said I needn't think my probation was over while I was working for him, and that he'd got his eye on me. He wanted to sack me.

ASPIN Go on.

GREEN-
HALGH I bet you I wouldn't have lasted three more days with him.

ASPIN I see.

(After a bit, Greenhalgh nods. He stands up and so does Aspin.)

ASPIN Well, it's too late to find out now.

GREEN-
HALGH Yes.

ASPIN What a mess. Why did you pick last night and not tonight, or tomorrow?

GREEN-
HALGH I felt depressed.

ASPIN I often feel depressed.

GREEN-
HALGH We had a little court martial in the kitchen. It was the first time my father had spoken to me for a week. He's bent an' all.

ASPIN And your Mother? Is she bent?

GREEN-
HALGH Well . . . she's . . .

ASPIN Bending?
(Greenhalgh nods.)
I feel sorry for the lot of them, don't you?

GREEN-
HALGH Not while they can push me about.

ASPIN That's not for long. You see you're making the mistake of thinking everybody's against you.

GREEN-
HALGH Wouldn't you?

ASPIN Yes, I would in your shoes—But I'd be wrong. Once you're through this bad patch, you'll find it's about fifty-fifty. Half for you. Half against. A working proposition anyway.

GREEN-
HALGH What'll happen when the cops come?

ASPIN You'll get punished. Unless you go to them.

GREEN-
HALGH What'll happen then?

ASPIN You'll still get punished.

GREEN-
HALGH What's the difference?

ASPIN If they catch you, they'll catch you like an animal. If you go to them, you'll walk like a man. Eh?

Outside the Baths

(Z Victor Two comes down the road and stops.)

Inside Z Victor Two

BAKER Z Victor Two to B.D. Off watch at the Blucher-Street Baths.

GIRL Thank you, Z Victor Two.

(Graham starts to get out of the car.)

One of the corridors in the Baths

(Greenhalgh and Aspin are leaving baths. At the foot of the staircase, they speak.)

GREEN-
HALGH Are you sure?

ASPIN You can take my word for it. It's the only way out. *(Terry looks reluctant.)* Nothing official, though. I've just told you what I think. You can please yourself.

(Greenhalgh thinks, looks down at the swimmers then . . .)

GREEN-
HALGH O.K.

(We see Greenhalgh and Aspin walking down the corridor towards the turnstile.)

Outside the Baths

(Graham is walking up and down at the entrance to the baths. Then a close shot of Baker looking at his watch.

As Greenhalgh and Aspin reach the main entrance, Baker gets out of the car and Graham approaches.)

GRAHAM Terry Greenhalgh?

GREEN-
HALGH Yes.
GRAHAM We'd like to ask you some questions in connection with damage
done in Mercer's Universal Stores last night. We'd like you to come
with us to the station.

(Nobody moves for a second. Then Greenhalgh kicks at the Probation Officer, turns and runs down the street. Graham and Baker chase after him. Aspin is left on the steps by himself.)

The C.I.D. office

(Barlow is sitting at his desk. Watt comes in, picks up the pile of papers he wanted and goes out.)

The Station office

TAYLOR Mr Mercer on the phone, sergeant. This is his third go.
WATT Tell him the law is taking its course.
TAYLOR Hello. Mr Mercer. I'm told to tell you that the law is taking its
course.

(Watt is pushing the papers into his briefcase.)

TAYLOR *(to Watt)* He says 'What the hell is that supposed to mean?'
WATT Give me that phone. Mr Mercer? Sergeant Watt here. It means we'll
stop at nothing to protect you and your property. That's what the
hell it's supposed to mean.

(Watt slams the phone down.)

And if he rings again, refer him to Inspector Barlow. I'm going to
spend the rest of me day off working at home.

(Watt leaves, snatching his hat and coat on the way out. Phone rings again.)

TAYLOR *(picking it up)* Sorry, Mr Mercer. I think you were cut off . . . No.
He's just left . . . Would Inspector Barlow do? . . . If I can get
him . . . Hold on please. *(He rings into Barlow.)*

The C.I.D. office

(Barlow picks up phone.)

BARLOW Chief Inspector . . . Put him on. *(pause)* Hello, Mr Mercer. Good
news. We've got the man . . . Sergeant Watt? . . . No . . . Why what
did he say? . . . Did he? . . . I'll deal with that without delay. Of
course, Mr Mercer . . . And let you know . . .

(Barlow puts down the phone and goes fast into outer office.)

The Station office

BARLOW Sergeant Watt?

TAYLOR Just left, sir.

(Barlow, seeing no hat and coat there, goes to the window behind the counter and throws it open. Outside Watt is just getting into his car.)

BARLOW Sergeant Watt. Can I see you a minute?

(Barlow slams the window and goes back into his office.)

A street in the town

(Greenhalgh is cornered. His clothes are torn. Graham and Baker overpower him and get him into the back of the car where Graham sits with him.)

The C.I.D. office

(Barlow is seated. Watt comes in.)

WATT Yes?

BARLOW 'Sir'. Sit down.

WATT Thank you, sir.

BARLOW That's better. *(Watt sits.)* Now, talk. *(Watt looks at him.)* I said talk. I don't like sulking. I don't like go-slows. I don't like exits and entrances and slamming doors. I don't like melodrama in any form. I said talk . . . go on.

WATT You're going to get your man half an hour earlier. You should be satisfied.

BARLOW Sergeant Watt, you can see I'm in a difficulty. I want you to explain things to me. Go on.

WATT I made a bargain with a Probation Officer. If he could get Greenhalgh to come in voluntarily, I was going to let him. For all I know he's kept his side of it. But I've not kept mine.

BARLOW That's your concern. Nothing to do with me.

WATT Aren't relations with the Probation Service your concern, sir?

BARLOW If a Probation Officer can't see that your loyalty's to your job, he's not fit to do his own.

WATT I was just trying to help the Probation Officer help the lad. I'm not trying to get him off.

BARLOW Then what are you doing?

WATT I'm trying to see him against his background.

BARLOW Give yourself a rest, John. Go with the system a bit. Lawbreaking is lawbreaking. It's not affected by background. If the magistrates want it to be, that's their concern. But not yours.

WATT Police work is detecting crime?

BARLOW Yes.

WATT	Finding suspects, breaking 'em down, running 'em in?
BARLOW	Yes.
WATT	At high speed?
BARLOW	At top speed.
WATT	And there's nothing more to it?
BARLOW	In this case, nothing.
WATT	Then if that's all, it's a job for barbarians.

(*Neither moves.*)

BARLOW   (*very deliberately*) Then you're a sergeant barbarian, Watt. That's not bad. And I'm an inspector barbarian. That's even better. Folk must take us as they find us.

The Station office

(*Greenhalgh is brought in by Graham and Baker. Very quiet.*)

GRAHAM   Greenhalgh to see Inspector Barlow.
TAYLOR   He's waiting.

(*Taylor picks up the phone.*)

C.I.D. office

(*Barlow picks up the phone.*)

BARLOW   Take him to the Interview Room. I'll be right out. (*He puts phone down.*) Another of our obligations, John. Unfailing courtesy to the public. Ring Mr Mercer. His number's on that pad. And tell him politely that we've made a charge—politely.

(*Barlow leaves the office.*)

The Interview Room

(*Greenhalgh is sitting without moving. Barlow comes in. His tone is genial.*)

BARLOW Well then lad. You are in a mess. Aren't you?

The C.I.D. office

Watt picks up phone and dials a number. As he does so, the picture fades out and the counter at Mercer's store fades in.

Running Milligan by Keith Dewhurst

The Cast

Detective Chief Inspector Barlow
Sergeant Blackitt
PC Jock Weir
PC Fancy Smith
PC David Graham
PC Ian Sweet
Betty, on duty in the Information Room
Freddie Milligan
Sandra, his young daughter
Cath, his sister-in-law
Jack, his brother-in-law
Mr Fletcher, his father-in-law
Milly, a prostitute
Ganger, who keeps an amusement arcade
An Attendant at the arcade
Coram, who keeps a lodging house
Harry, a rag-and-bone man who lives there
Alderman Wilson

Running Milligan

The main gates of a prison

(*We are inside the main gate. The small wicket gate opens. Milligan and a Warder are silhouetted in the opening. Milligan steps out. The camera follows him through the wicket gate. He hesitates at the unexpected traffic noise, and turns back into a full-fact close-up. He hears the wicket bang shut, and then slowly turns back. The camera does not move as he walks out of view.*)

Inside Z Victor One

(*Jock and Fancy have stopped for a smoke, which they are just finishing.*)

FANCY Hey.

JOCK What?

FANCY We'd best get on.

JOCK Aye. I suppose we had. (*He blows a final cloud of smoke, and starts the engine.*)

A busy street

(*The camera shows us a tobacconist's window with the usual varied display. We cut to a close-up of Milligan looking in, and then a wider shot showing what Milligan sees. The shopgirl bends to get something from under the counter. Milligan is watching her. The shopgirl realises she is being watched. She straightens up and turns to look at Milligan, but Milligan cannot match her stare.*

Cut to a shot from the edge of the pavement: Milligan turns, comes towards the camera, and steps off the pavement without looking. The sudden noise of a horn and brakes. Z Victor One almost runs him down. The car moves on. Milligan half runs across the rest of the roadway.)

Inside Z Victor One

FANCY By heck.

(*Jock is still watching Milligan.*)

JOCK Aye.

FANCY Nice bit of braking, though.

JOCK (*turning*) Mmm.

FANCY Like I said to my girlie last night. I've got sensitive hands and feet, darling, that's what I've got.

JOCK That feller.

FANCY He'll die young.

JOCK I know him.

FANCY Eh?

JOCK Robbery with violence. He hit some old man on the head.

FANCY Old man?

JOCK Milligan.

FANCY What are you talking about?

JOCK Freddy Milligan.

FANCY Freddy Milligan. Yes. A right villain. What about him?

JOCK That was him walked off the pavement.

FANCY No.

JOCK It was.

FANCY Never. He's in Walton.

JOCK Are you sure?

FANCY Well, he got a long stretch, Jock. Five years or—

JOCK (*reaching for the radio*) I'm going to check it.

FANCY Come on. If he's escaped we'd have heard.

JOCK I'm checking.

FANCY That bloke was in civvies.

JOCK Z Victor One for BD . . .

A street

(*The picture dissolves to a shot of Milligan walking along the streets.*)

The Information Room

BETTY Thank you Z Tango Three, your message timed at 8.23. BD for Z Victor One.

BETTY Z Victor One. Reference your query. Frederick Joseph Milligan was released on parole from Walton Prison this morning. We understand him to be attending the funeral of his wife.

Inside Z Victor One

JOCK Thank you BD. Roger.

FANCY Well done.

JOCK Shut up.

FANCY Released on parole.

JOCK	I'll bet it was him.
FANCY	Very likely.
JOCK	Not much though, is it? Getting out for a funeral.
FANCY	Oh. I don't know.
JOCK	Eh?
FANCY	It's better than getting out for a wedding.
JOCK	For why?
FANCY	Frustration: one kiss—back again.
JOCK	You've got a smutty mind, d'you know that?
FANCY	Smut yourself. He shouldn't have coshed the old man, should he? Eh?

Building site

(We see the back of Milligan's head with a block of flats in background. The camera pans Right as he turns and sees a second block of flats.
Cut to a shot looking down at Milligan in the centre of the building site. He goes up to a group of workmen with a piece of paper. A work-man points to Hazelwood Towers, one of the blocks of flats, and Milligan starts to walk towards it.)

Living room of one of the flats

(This is the living room of the flat which Milligan is seeking. The furnishings are not as clean and modern as the lines of the flat itself.
Cath, Milligan's sister-in-law, is lighting a woodbine. She is in her mid-thirties, and rather worn.
There is a knock.)

CATH	*(calling)* It's on the latch.
	(Cath moves as the door opens.)

115

CATH (*stopping*) **Oh.**
(*We cut and see that Milligan is there.*)
MILLIGAN **Cath.**
(*They stare at each other.*)
CATH I'll make some tea.

The kitchen

(*Cath turns back and starts to make the tea. Milligan follows.*)

CATH You found it then.
MILLIGAN Yes. (*He is looking round for something.*) It's high up, isn't it?
CATH Yes.
MILLIGAN Got a lift though, eh?
CATH When it's working.
MILLIGAN Oh. (*He turns to face her.*) I—I appreciate what you've done, Cath. I want you to know. I'll pay you back, like. I'll see you right when it's—well—when—
(*He sees what he has been looking for: cigarettes. We see a close-up of the packet and then pan up to a close-up of Milligan. Cut to a shot of Cath, who is watching him take one.*)
MILLIGAN We don't get many inside. You know.
CATH Keep the packet.
MILLIGAN That's my smiling Cath, eh?
CATH Shut up.
MILLIGAN Aye. Aye: well: where's the rest of 'em?
CATH Jack's at work. I sent my father out.
MILLIGAN Oh. They're all right, I mean, you know they're . . . ?
(*She stares. He shrugs and turns away.*)

CATH	I've got things to say to you.
MILLIGAN	Aye. Aye. It's the traffic that's done it, of course. Given me this headache. You know. Like that window cleaning job. My eyes just went funny with staring at glass. People wouldn't believe it, I mean, but, well, you know me, I mean—
CATH	Yes. You married my sister.
MILLIGAN	Aye. (*They stare.*)
CATH	That's one of the things, Freddy.
MILLIGAN	What?
CATH	The undertaker feller. He said, where d'you want her to be, you know.
MILLIGAN	Aye.
CATH	We've too many kids in the house.
MILLIGAN	Eh?
CATH	We said we'd have her at the funeral parlour.
MILLIGAN	Oh.
CATH	It's got up like a church.
MILLIGAN	Oh.
CATH	You know.
MILLIGAN	I wouldn't have thought that of you, Cath. I wouldn't.

The living room

(*Milligan wanders in. Cath stands in the doorway.*)

MILLIGAN	Your own sister, I mean. Margaret. She should have been lying at home.
CATH	She didn't have no home.
MILLIGAN	I know. I know that.
CATH	She got chucked out because you were in prison and she'd no money.
MILLIGAN	Yes.
CATH	So now your kiddies have no mam and—
MILLIGAN	I said thank you.
CATH	And you've no home.
MILLIGAN	I mean, you and Jack, you've been wonderful. You have. You've . . . (*He stops as they both realise they are being observed. They look. It is Sandra, Milligan's small daughter, who has just come in.*)
SANDRA	Dad. (*She runs into his kneeling embrace. She starts to cry.*)
MILLIGAN	Don't cry, girlie. Don't cry.
CATH	Why aren't you at school?
SANDRA	I didn't want.
CATH	You . . .
SANDRA	Have you come for me?

MILLIGAN Sandra . . .

SANDRA Have you?

(Cath sighs but is determined.)

CATH I want to know, Freddy.

MILLIGAN Eh?

CATH What is going to happen when you get out?

MILLIGAN I'm telling you—

SANDRA She hates me.

MILLIGAN No.

SANDRA She does.

CATH Sandra.

SANDRA She says I'm like my mother was.

MILLIGAN There y'are. She—

SANDRA She says I'm like her because I can get men.

CATH You're like your father because you tell lies.

SANDRA Daddy.

MILLIGAN I'm—I'm telling your Auntie Cath, love. It's like I'm trying t tell her. *(He disengages Sandra's arms.)* I've got this headache, yo see.

Newtown Police Station

(Barlow is at the desk, waving a letter at Blackitt, who is counterin with an item on a clip-file.)

BARLOW Look. It happens hundreds of times every day. There's a ca driving along, when some fool steps off the pavement.

BLACKITT Yes, sir.

BARLOW By luck or management there's no accident. They both continu

118

BLACKITT I know, sir. Yes. It was Freddy—

BARLOW Never mind that. The difference is that when it happened on Seaport High Street yesterday morning, Alderman blooming Wilson J.P. just happened to be looking out of the window of his furnishing store. As a result of which he's written me this letter.

BLACKITT Yes, sir, I—

BARLOW (reading) '. . . no doubt the registration number of the relevant vehicle will be of interest, especially in view of the status of the highway in question . . . '

BLACKITT Accident Zone. Yes, sir.

BARLOW It's Z Victor One.

BLACKITT Yes sir.

BARLOW What do you mean: yes?

BLACKITT I'm trying to explain, sir. The feller who stepped off the pavement was Freddy Milligan.

BARLOW Milligan's inside.

BLACKITT With you being off yesterday, sir, you—

BARLOW Wait a minute, if Milligan's escaped and Smith and Weir . . .

BLACKITT He's on parole, sir.

BARLOW Oh.

BLACKITT Wife's funeral. (Barlow sighs.) Wier thought he recognised him and—

BARLOW I know. He radioed BD. BD telephoned Walton and a lot of time and public money went down the drain because it isn't considered fair to furnish the police with the names of men on parole.

BLACKITT Yes.

BARLOW It's ridiculous.

BLACKITT Yes, sir.

BARLOW Parole itself. Well meant, but ridiculous.

BLACKITT Er . . .

BARLOW Come on. You know it is.

BLACKITT Yes. But, I mean, if you were Milligan—

BARLOW I'm not though, am I?

BLACKITT No, sir.

BARLOW No. When does his sentence expire?

BLACKITT Er—next month, sir.

BARLOW Good. He's not likely to do anything daft.

BLACKITT No sir.

BARLOW Unlike Smith and Weir.

BLACKITT Er . . .

BARLOW I want them. Here.

A cemetery

(We see a single high shot of Milligan and a few relatives who form a small party round the grave.)

The kitchen that evening

(Cath and her husband Jack are in the doorway. Beyond them we can see Milligan in the living room. Sandra is by him. Mr Fletcher, Cath's father, is also in the living room, where other children are running about and the TV is on.)

JACK You did tell him?

CATH Yes.

JACK I mean, you put it straight? *(Cath sighs impatiently.)* All right.

CATH What d'you mean: all right?

The living room

(Simply a close-up of Milligan. The other conversation continues, and we hear Jack's voice, echoing.)

JACK I mean I paid for the funeral and all that, but he's your family, isn't he? They're your sister's kids and you said you'd take 'em in.

The kitchen

CATH It was for the time being.

JACK I hope he knows it.

CATH You're scared of him, aren't you?

JACK Eh?

CATH You're scared, but I'm not, you see, I—
(She breaks off, suddenly aware that Milligan has stood up and is watching them.)

MILLIGAN I'm going out.
(*Cath looks exhausted.*)

The living room

(*A close-up of Milligan.*)
JACK I'll—er—buy you a pint if you like, Fred.
MILLIGAN No.
JACK You've got time.
MILLIGAN No.
(*He stares for a split second and then goes. A wide shot shows them all frozen with surprise. Then Sandra starts to move.*)
SANDRA (*calling*) Daddy.
CATH Sandra.
SANDRA Shut your face, you!
JACK Hey—
SANDRA Dad . . . (*she is out of the room.*)

The landing outside the flat

(*Milligan gets into the lift and goes down. We hear the voices from above.*)
SANDRA Dad.
JACK Sandra!
(*The voices are cut off and Milligan's face is held in the camera.*)

Outside the flats

(*It is nearly dark. The blocks of flats are bulky black outlines. There are lights here and there, and faint traffic noise.*)
SANDRA (*faintly as if in the distance*) Don't go. Don't leave me.

Outside the prison

(*It is night. We see a still photo of the prison, but hear Sandra's voice over; it has a metallic echo, wailing.*)

SANDRA Don't leave me.

A street by night

(*We see Milligan in a brief close-up, the headlights of a car flaring over his face.*)

The Information Room

BETTY BD for Z Victor One . . . BD for Z Victor One.

JOCK (*whose distorted voice is heard over the wireless telephone*) Z Victor One. Sorry, love.
(*During Betty's dictation of the message, the picture slowly mixes to show us Milligan, walking along the street.*)

BETTY Z Victor One. Go to 38 Jackson Court, Newtown Parkway, Newtown, to interview the family of Frederick Joseph Milligan, who has failed to honour his parole from Walton Prison. He should have reported back at twenty hundred hours. He is believed to have been staying at Jackson Court with his sister-in-law, Mrs Catherine Woods.

Inside Z Victor One.

JOCK Thank you BD. Roger. (*He replaces his receiver.*) Well?

FANCY Eh?

JOCK Don't tell me you're surprised.

FANCY Jackson Court, was it?

JOCK I mean, when I saw Milligan yesterday—

FANCY Newtown Parkway.

JOCK I could see then—

FANCY You'd be better occupied wondering what Barlow wants us for.

JOCK Oh, that.

FANCY Yes.

JOCK Never mind it. When I looked at Milligan there was something there then. You know. At the back of his eyes.

FANCY Aye. His skull.

A street

(*Milligan in close-up, the camera tracking back with him as he walks. His breath is loud and jerky.*)

Newtown Police Station

(Barlow is in the foreground with one telephone, Sweet with another. Blackitt is in the background with a third.)

BARLOW *(on the phone)* Yes. Yes. We'll do all that.

SWEET *(on the phone)* I see. Thank you. *(He hangs up and starts to come across to Barlow.)*

BARLOW *(on the phone)* You're what? Oh. Yes, of course. *(He hangs up.)* He's panicking. Should we get Milligan's picture on television?

BLACKITT Smashing.

BARLOW I don't think.

SWEET Nothing from the hospital, sir. Nothing from the Ambulance Service.

BARLOW No. Try the buses.

SWEET Eh?

BARLOW He may have been on one that broke down.

SWEET Oh.

(He retires to the phone again. Blackitt has now hung up.)

BLACKITT Very thorough.

BARLOW Eh?

BLACKITT I'm in the process of flashing my police pillars, sir, most of the men know Milligan by sight; they'll keep a watch on public houses—

BARLOW Yes.

BLACKITT I'm also arranging for two men to go to the bus station, sir, and two to the long distance lorry park—

BARLOW Yes. You'll do it very well. *(Blackitt opts for silence.)* While we're strung out looking for Milligan there'll be half a dozen break-ins going unsolved, won't there? Hmmm?

BLACKITT It's a funeral.

BARLOW Yes.

BLACKITT Aye. Well. Be over at the house, will you, sir?

BARLOW Yes.

BLACKITT D'you think he had anything organised?

BARLOW Do you? *(Blackitt shrugs.)* You might well shrug.

(Barlow is going, but Blackitt checks him.)

BLACKITT I just think I'd like to be there.

BARLOW Eh?

BLACKITT You know. If it was my wife.

(We see Barlow's reaction.)

The living room of the Woods' flat

(Fancy Smith and Jock Weir are questioning Jack and Cath. Mr Fletcher is

still sitting, and two or three children, Sandra among them, are watching
from the kitchen door.)

FANCY   Right. Milligan had to report back at eight. He didn't need t
leave here until seven, but in fact he got up and walked out a
twenty-five to.

JACK   Yes.

FANCY   Did you ask him where he was going?

MR FLETCHER   Did they heck.

FANCY   Why not?

JACK   I said I'd buy him a beer. He said no, so I . . .

CATH   We thought he'd just have a walk and then—

JACK   Yes.

JOCK   Did he have any money?

JACK   There was a pound or two from what his wife had.

FANCY   Did you give him any?

CATH   No.

FANCY   Did he steal any?

CATH   No.

JOCK   How d'you know?

CATH   I've looked.

JOCK   Oh.

FANCY   How long did he stay here altogether?

JACK   Well, it was a thirty-six hours, like . . .

JOCK   Did he go out?

JACK   Well—

FANCY   By himself.

CATH   Yes.

JOCK   Where to?

CATH   Cigarettes. You know.

JOCK   Is that all?

JACK   Ah, well, I was at work, you see, I—

FANCY   When did he go out, how long did he stay?

CATH   Fifteen minutes.

JOCK   Then what did he do all day?

CATH   Nothing. He just sat there.

FANCY   Did he go out with any of you?

JACK   Certainly.

FANCY   What for?

JACK   Funeral.

FANCY   Who was there?

MR FLETCHER   Nobody.

FANCY   Eh?

MR FLETCHER	I couldn't get. There was nobody. Buried, with nobody there.
CATH	Shut up.
JOCK	What d'you mean? Nobody?
FLETCHER	You'd best ask her.
CATH	Er—this morning. Fred went out this morning.
FANCY	Oh?
CATH	He stood by the children's playground.
FANCY	Where's that?
	(*Cath points down and out of the window.*)
JOCK	Did he talk to anybody?
CATH	How do I know?
JACK	No. No. He wouldn't have. He didn't with me.
FANCY	You?
JACK	I bought him a drink.
FANCY	Public house?
JACK	Yes. He didn't talk. 'Course he didn't know nobody.
JOCK	What?
JACK	We've been rehoused, you see. New people.
JOCK	Oh.
JACK	I'm from the Pool anyway.
CATH	I mean, normally, we don't see Freddy.
JACK	We didn't live near, you see. The Milligans are all Seaport.
FANCY	Are they?
JACK	'Course they are. I mean, if you think Fred fixed something up with somebody he met here . . .
CATH	He'd never been here before.
FANCY	No?
JACK	No. Seaport, whack. That's your best bet. Seaport.

Street near the docks

(*Milligan standing, looking round with no particular certainty at his home ground. Ship's sirens can be heard.*)

The kitchen

(*Barlow has arrived and is discussing the position with Weir. The others are in the living room.*)

BARLOW	I've talked to the hospital. Mrs Milligan had been in for three weeks. They knew she'd die but it happened much quicker than they expected.
JOCK	What was wrong with her?
BARLOW	Cancer.

JOCK Oh.

BARLOW Anyway, you'd better check with that newsagent who sold him the cigarettes.

JOCK Yes, sir.

(*Barlow is ready to move.*)

You know, when I spotted Milligan in the street, sir, I thought there was—

BARLOW Oh yes.

JOCK I beg your pardon sir?

BARLOW Nothing, Weir, nothing.

JOCK Oh.

BARLOW For the moment.

(*Jock is still slightly puzzled but Barlow sweeps him on.*)

Now get on. Then wait for me downstairs.

JOCK Right sir.

The living room

(*We cut as Barlow and Jock come out of the kitchen.*)

JOCK Come on.

FANCY Right.

(*Fancy and Jock go.*)

JACK Hey—are they . . . ?

BARLOW Newsagent.

JACK Oh.

BARLOW Yes. Well. It doesn't look as though Milligan had the time to fix anything up, really.

JACK Oh.

BARLOW Unless you helped him, of course.

JACK Eh?

MR FLETCHER Help him? They wouldn't help him out of a pullover.

CATH Shut your face.

MR FLETCHER Why should I?

CATH Because why should we help him? That's why. Why should we?

MR FLETCHER He's family.

CATH He's no good.

MR FLETCHER Are you any better?

JACK Now wait a—

CATH And just what d'you mean by that?

MR FLETCHER You know very well what I mean. You fancied him yourself, and when—

CATH Shut up.

JACK Cath—

MR FLETCHER What one woman can't have she won't let anybody else—

CATH Shut up.

JACK Cath, I—

CATH And you.

(There is silence. Too late, they remember Barlow.)

BARLOW I'm sorry. I should have put my question in another way.

JACK What?

BARLOW If you won't help Freddy to run away, what will you help him to do? Eh?

A street

(Milligan is outside a house. He hesitates, looks round, and goes in.)

The living room

BARLOW Well?

JACK Well: you know . . .

BARLOW You mean: you don't want to help him at all?

JACK No. No, I—

MR FLETCHER You're a custard. That's what you are.

CATH Leave him alone.

MR FLETCHER Ah . . .

BARLOW Look. You think it's your problem. I see it every day. One man like Milligan can destroy the happiness of an entire family. Very likely he doesn't mean to: but he does, because of what he is.

JACK Aye. He does.

BARLOW So what happened, then?

JACK Oh. I suppose you'd say that—

127

CATH How d'you mean, mister? 'What happened?'

JACK Cath—

CATH I want to hear.

BARLOW I think you know already, love.

(*Barlow and Cath stare.*)

All right. Freddy didn't make any plans in prison because his wife died too suddenly. He didn't make any here. You didn't make any for him.

CATH No.

BARLOW No. Other men have made plans, so we have to check, just in case, even when we think it hasn't happened.

JACK Eh?

BARLOW I've told you. It's common. A man comes out on parole and if he thinks it's going to be a little bit of freedom he's wrong. It isn't. Leaving prison's painful. It's like leaving your bed for the first time when you've had a leg amputated. But that's not all he has to face. Oh no. They've let him out for a heartbreaking like his wife's funeral.

MR FLETCHER I should hope so.

BARLOW Would you?

MR FLETCHER Yes.

BARLOW Yes, and maybe you're tough, but Freddy isn't, is he?

MR FLETCHER He's all right.

BARLOW I sent him down. He's as weak as water. He's due out in six weeks and I thought that might save him, but no, he's cracked. Why? What happened?

CATH Ask him.

BARLOW I'm asking you. What are you feeling ashamed about?

CATH What?

BARLOW Don't—er—don't you think it's time the children went to bed?

CATH Eh?

(*Barlow jerks his head at the children.*)

Oh. Oh yes. Go on.

(*They go, except for Sandra.*)

What are you staring at?

(*Sandra goes: sullen.*)

BARLOW You do feel a bit ashamed, don't you?

CATH No.

BARLOW Come on.

CATH What's it to you?

BARLOW Nothing. I might just catch him quicker if I know what he's thinking. That's all.

CATH   All right.

BARLOW   Is it?

CATH   All right. I told him.

BARLOW   Told him what?

CATH   I—I told him that when he comes out of prison, see, when he— he can take his kids and get out. Out. All of 'em.

BARLOW   I see.

CATH   Do you?

BARLOW   Yes. Every day of the week.

CATH   All right.

JACK   You can see, can't you? Fred's no money, he's no—what other way is there?

BARLOW   Be quiet. You'll keep the children until he does come out?

CATH   What do you think?

BARLOW   I think that if I twisted their arms the Welfare people might find you a bigger flat.

CATH   No.

BARLOW   Why not?

CATH   We can't afford it.

BARLOW   I'll send 'em round anyway.

CATH   Thank you for nothing.

BARLOW   It's not for you, you know.

CATH   No: and it's not for Margaret neither, is it?

BARLOW   Eh?

CATH   She's dead, isn't she? She's dead is old Margaret. She's not sick of it all day, is she? I'm not hurting her one little bit, am I? (*Silence: which Barlow breaks with a sigh.*)

BARLOW   All right. I'll arrange for statements to be taken tomorrow.

(He is making for the door. He opens it.)

MR FLETCHER Have—er—have you got children, mister?

BARLOW Yes. I might put a man downstairs, by the way, in case Freddy doubles back.

JACK Oh.

(Barlow nods and goes.)

MR FLETCHER I had five girls.

JACK I know.

MR FLETCHER Aye.

(Jack is looking at Cath, trying to get a response: but Cath is just staring.) Five.

JACK Yes.

MR FLETCHER I can't honestly say I liked any of 'em, really.

(Cath goes on working, and working, and we close in for a close-up.)

Inside Z Victor One

(The car is parked. Barlow is in the back seat, briefing Fancy and Jock.)

BARLOW Same old story. Ninety-nine out of a hundred of every failure to honour parole. He's weak. He can't cope. He's got his life in a mess so he did what he always does.

JOCK He ran away.

BARLOW Yes.

FANCY He could be clear by now.

BARLOW No. He'll go to the people he knows.

JOCK Well, yes, sir, but if he's no money . . .

BARLOW It's what he'll do, Weir. I know. I can feel him.

JOCK Yes sir.

BARLOW Get me Criminal Records on that thing.

FANCY Yes sir. *(He lifts the radio, and speaks.)* Z Victor One for BD.

BARLOW He's like all excuse-makers, Weir. He's got to persuade himsel first.

FANCY Hello. Z Victor One. Hello.

BARLOW And that means Seaport. His old pals. The people who'll sit and listen while Milligan talks to himself.

Milly's room

(Milly is a middle-aged prostitute. The room is in a large decrepit house. In the background we hear the faint noise of radios, arguments, etc. Milly is getting dressed and made-up to go out. Milligan is watching and talking.)

MILLIGAN So I thought why not? No harm is there? I mean, no harm in my coming up here.

MILLY No.

MILLIGAN People lose touch. I know.

MILLY Yes.

MILLIGAN 'Course that's life. I've lost my Margaret, and . . .

MILLY Sudden.

MILLIGAN Nothing wrong with her. Collapsed in the street. Next time I saw her she was dead. I couldn't believe it. You know. Nothing in my mind except—well—but no. The doctor said no, Mr Milligan, he said, no, no, there's no pain with it.

MILLY Oh.

MILLIGAN There's just a kind of a—well—like cracking your head on a cupboard door: and that's it.

MILLY Oh.

MILLIGAN It's those left behind that have the pain.

MILLY Yes.

MILLIGAN You know, don't you?

MILLY Anyway: it wasn't cancer.

MILLIGAN Eh?

MILLY Cancer.

MILLIGAN It wasn't.

MILLY I know. I'm saying. I can't stand it, you know. I just can't listen to a cancer story.

MILLIGAN No. I remember.

MILLY It's my secret fear is cancer.

MILLIGAN Yes. Yes, anyway, it's Cath, actually, you see.

MILLY Cath?

MILLIGAN My sister-in-law. You remember. She's never liked me.

MILLY Oh.

MILLIGAN I mean, that time I had the window-cleaning round. Bad winter. I couldn't get out. We needed a few quid to tide us over, but no, no, not Cath. Same as the funeral.

MILLY What?

MILLIGAN Well, I've no savings, have I?

MILLY No.

MILLIGAN I can see Cath's point in one way, of course. In another—well, the children I mean. The children must be my principal worry, mustn't they? If I'm not there, and—and where am I going to go, and—

MILLY Well. You can't come here, can you?
(She gets up and starts rummaging in the wardrobe. Her open handbag has been left behind at the dressing table.)

MILLIGAN No. No, I—

MILLY I mean, I'm carrying on my business here.

MILLIGAN Yes.

MILLY Was she all white?
(Milligan's hand is half in the handbag.)

MILLIGAN Eh?

MILLY Your Margaret. White wedding.

MILLIGAN Oh. Er—yes. She was. All white.

MILLY Very nice.

MILLIGAN Honeymoon at New Brighton.

MILLY Oh.

MILLIGAN Friday to Monday.

MILLY Well: you've got the remembrance, haven't you?
(She turns back. Milligan has taken the money.)

MILLIGAN She—er—she was a very pure girl, you know.

MILLY Was she?

MILLIGAN She wasn't like you.

MILLY Thank you.

MILLIGAN I mean, she didn't have the understanding.

MILLY I'll bet you were sorry when your mother died, weren't you?

MILLIGAN Eh?
(Milly is ready to go. She finally picks up the handbag.)

MILLY Did you leave me my fare to Lime Street?

MILLIGAN What?

MILLY *(she feels the odd coins)* You did. Come on.

MILLIGAN Milly—

MILLY *(opening the door)* You're a bad liar, Freddy. Now get on your way.
(Milligan looks: bangs his fist in anger: walks out.)
Oh well. Don't mention it then.
(She goes herself.)

(*Barlow is completing his instructions to Fancy and Jock. At the moment he is speaking to H.Q. on the wireless-telephone.*)

BARLOW (*to radio*) Right. Thank you. (*He hands the phone to Fancy to hook up.*) Got your pencil?

JOCK Yes sir.

BARLOW Millicent Jackson. Known as Milly. Prostitute. She lives in King Terrace and works the pubs around Lime Street. We charged her with receiving after one of Milligan's jobs but the magistrate wouldn't listen.

JOCK D'you think she'd hide him, sir?

BARLOW No. She needs the room, but check it anyway. Then the lodging houses. Salvation Army. Seaport Municipal.

JOCK Yes sir.

BARLOW Then Coram's.

FANCY Coram's?

BARLOW Old Harry Smith.

FANCY Oh, aye.

BARLOW Yes. Everybody's favourite informer. I'll get Liverpool City to check on the other relatives and then I'm going to see the Ganger.

FANCY Right sir.

(*Barlow is getting out.*)

JOCK Sir.

BARLOW What?

JOCK Will you ask Liverpool City to look for the Jackson woman?

BARLOW Er—I will. Yes.

JOCK Right sir.

(*Barlow is out, but puts his head back.*)

BARLOW And, Weir . . .

JOCK Sir?

BARLOW While we're all reminding one another.

JOCK Sir?

BARLOW I still want to see you two.

The living room

(*Cath is sitting abstracted. Jack trying to talk to her.*)

JACK Cath. (*There is no reply.*) Cath.

CATH Shut up.

JACK I must know, Cath. I mean, I don't mind. I just want to know.

CATH Know what?

JACK Freddy.

CATH   Oh.

JACK   Did you.

CATH   Did I what?

JACK   (*He cannot match her stare.*) 'Course, as you say, when he's inside we're better off.

CATH   It doesn't matter then, does it?

JACK   Eh?

CATH   It doesn't matter. Nothing's ever right. So nothing matters. Does it?

An amusement arcade by night

(*The arcade is merely an ordinary shop with a few pin tables and machines and a small shooting gallery at the back end. It is very seedy. Not a great deal of business is being done. The window is steamy. Pop music is being played.*

Milligan is making his way in and up to the shooting gallery. The attendant, who is in his very early twenties, is leaning on the counter. A door in the side wall beyond the counter leads to the office, which is behind the gallery itself. The attendant pushes a rifle at Milligan.)

ATTENDANT   Five for a shilling.

MILLIGAN   No.

ATTENDANT   Then clear off.

MILLIGAN   George.

ATTENDANT   Eh? (*He sees it is Milligan.*) Oh. It's you.

MILLIGAN   I see you've got my old job.

ATTENDANT   What d'you want?

MILLIGAN   The Ganger.

ATTENDANT   Oh.

MILLIGAN   Is he in?

ATTENDANT   I'll have to look. Won't I?

(*He goes through the door. Milligan picks up the gun. It makes him feel pretty big. He fires it. The attendant reappears.*)

ATTENDANT   Milligan.

MILLIGAN   I knew it. (*He ducks under the flap and goes through the door.*)

The Ganger's office

(*The office is small and very full: broken machines, old chairs, box files, rolls of lino, a safe, a gas-ring, kettle and cups.*

Ganger himself is on the fat side and has a suit, a none too clean shirt and a flashy tie clip. He keeps his hat on. He has a roll top desk jammed against the wall and is in his swivel chair, which he wheels to face Milligan. He has an open parcel of chips on the desk.)

MILLIGAN Hello. Ganger.
GANGER Frederick.
(*Milligan shuffles. Ganger offers a chip.*) Have you brought your vinegar?
MILLIGAN No. No. I'm—I'm on the run, Ganger. (*Ganger swivels: his back is to Milligan.*) I'm giving you the straight gen, you see: it's a funny business, I—

GANGER Don't.
MILLIGAN Eh?
GANGER Don't Frederick. I don't want to know. (*We just see Milligan's reaction before cutting to:*)

Milly's room

(*The room is empty. Jock and Fancy are outside, knocking.*)
FANCY (*heard through the door*) Come on. Open up. Police.
(*Fancy groans. There is a fiddling with the lock, then a decisive shove. They burst in. The light goes on to show Fancy admiring the knife with which he has flipped back the lock.*)
FANCY I told you. I'd have made a right safecracker.
JOCK You shouldn't have done it.
FANCY Milly Jackson. Prostitute. What's she going to say?
JOCK He's not here anyway.
FANCY No.
JOCK Then let's get out.
FANCY (*making no move*) Aye.
JOCK (*at the door*) Fancy.
FANCY It's funny you know.

JOCK For goodness sake.

FANCY I never really thought about Milligan until I saw this room.

JOCK Well I did

FANCY If it was your wife, Jock. If you were the one coming out of Walton—

JOCK It's all the same now, son. It's as though he'd broken out.

FANCY Aye. That's what makes it ridiculous.

Ganger's office

(*The conversation between Ganger and Milligan is punctuated by the crack of rifles, and the noise of bullets hitting the other side of the wall.*)

MILLIGAN It's all going through my mind, you see. It's like pictures of my past life, I mean, I might drop dead tomorrow, I—I need fresh air, fresh start, think it all over—

GANGER You come in here. You show your face to the whole clientele.

MILLIGAN I've lost my wife, Ganger.

GANGER You've no money.

MILLIGAN No. I've four pound ten.

GANGER Go on, Frederick. Rub me all over with itching powder.

MILLIGAN No. No. I mean, that little Welsh feller that time. He had no money.

GANGER (*groaning*) Oh . . .

MILLIGAN We helped him. Put him on the B and I boat. You and me.

GANGER They weren't looking for him.

MILLIGAN They were.

GANGER Nobody knew his name. Nobody had his picture.

MILLIGAN I've thought about you, Ganger. You know.

GANGER Aye. Then think again.

MILLIGAN Eh?

GANGER You're catalogued. They're not looking for some man. Unseen. They're looking for you.

(*Milligan is silent. A shot pings from the arcade.*)

MILLIGAN Don't it get on your nerves?

GANGER Eh?

MILLIGAN The shooting.

GANGER Go away.

MILLIGAN 'Course, I suppose if I did have money—

GANGER Yes. It would be. Amazing.

MILLIGAN Eh?

GANGER Amazing. The way people rushed to help.

MILLIGAN	Aye.
GANGER	(*after a pause*) That's been one of your troubles, though, hasn't it?
MILLIGAN	What?
GANGER	No access to funds.
MILLIGAN	Aye. (*Silence.*) Aye. Well. Happy days then, Ganger.
GANGER	Aye. (*Milligan is going. Ganger checks him.*) And—er—you know.
MILLIGAN	Eh?
GANGER	Your wife. Deepest sympathy.
MILLIGAN	Oh. Yes. Thank you. Thank you very much.

(*He goes. Ganger sighs. Removes his hat and finds his rosary among the chip paper. He goes down on one knee, crossing himself. The attendant comes in.*)

ATTENDANT	That Milligan's got the cheek of—
GANGER	Go away.
ATTENDANT	Eh?
GANGER	You heard.
ATTENDANT	Oh.
GANGER	No. On second thoughts. Get down.
ATTENDANT	Oh. (*He kneels.*)
GANGER	Commencing with 'Now and at the hour of our death.'
ATTENDANT	Right. (*We hear the mutter of prayer, gunfire, and pop music.*) Hey.
GANGER	What?
ATTENDANT	Who's it for?
GANGER	Milligan's wife.
ATTENDANT	Oh.

(*More prayer accompanied by gunfire.*
Barlow appears in the doorway behind them. He stares, amazedly. Then knocks and withdraws a little, but the attendant has spotted him.)

ATTENDANT Ganger.

GANGER Shut up.

ATTENDANT It's Barlow.

GANGER Eh?

ATTENDANT Barlow. You know.

GANGER Oh.

(*He rises. The attendant makes to follow but Ganger keeps him down with an arm on the shoulder.*) You stick at it. You've got a more innocent mind than me.

(*He goes to the door.*)

The amusement arcade

(*Barlow is helping himself to a rifle and five. Ganger appears. Barlow fires.*)

BARLOW Ganger.

GANGER Mr Barlow. (*Barlow stares—Ganger meets it.*) We just—er—well—I won't tell you a lie. We just heard of the death of a friend.

BARLOW Oh.

GANGER In the midst of life, Mr Barlow.

BARLOW Aye. (*He shows the rifle.*) I thought I'd take five. You don't mind, do you?

Newtown Police Station

(*Blackitt is on the phone to Z Victor One. Sweet is near, and Alderman Wilson is on the other side of the desk.*)

BLACKITT (*to phone*) Hello. Hello.

Smith? Yes. Is Mr Barlow still with you? Then where is he? Oh. Well, if you see him first there's a message. We've got Alderman Wilson here. He—er—he was a witness in a traffic incident. Mr Barlow knows the facts. Yes. Right. (*Blackitt puts down the phone.*)

Well, sir if you care to wait you're welcome, but personally I—

WILSON I will wait. Thank you.

BLACKITT Right sir.

WILSON That's what I'm saying. The point must be made.

BLACKITT Yes sir.

WILSON They must crack down. They must show they mean business. Verb sap.

BLACKITT Beg pardon, sir?

WILSON A word to the wise. We hope it'll be sufficient, don't we?

A street near the docks

(*We are looking down a little on Milligan, who walks a few paces towards the camera and then looks up. We cut to what Milligan sees:*

The battered fanlight, lit from inside, and showing the letters—CORAM'S LODGING HOUSE.)

Outside the lodging house door

(*This scene is shot from just outside Coram's open door, looking through it into the dim passage hall, and at the stairs. Milligan pulls the bell. It jangles at the back of the house.*)

CORAM (*shouting from the back*) Full up.

(*Milligan pulls the bell again. Coram appears at the end of the hall. Milligan leans back into the shadow.*)

CORAM I said I'm—where are you?

MILLIGAN Coram.

CORAM Come into the light, cocky.

MILLIGAN I was wondering about Old Harry, Mr Coram.
CORAM Oh?
MILLIGAN I'd like a gas with him. You know.
CORAM I'm full up.
MILLIGAN He used to doss here, didn't he, I mean—
CORAM Who are you, cocky: the back legs of the horse?
MILLIGAN No. I'm Harry's nephew, actually.
CORAM (*almost at the door*) Are you?
MILLIGAN Yes. Well. Bad luck. Family bereavement. Blood's thicker than water, in't it, I mean—
(*As Milligan moves we cut to:*

Inside the lodging house

(*Milligan is cruelly fast. He punches Coram in the stomach and bundles him inside, holding him up against the wall.*)
MILLIGAN I hate you, Coram.
(*Coram cannot get his breath.*)
Shut up.
(*Coram tries to speak.*)
Where's Harry?
(*Coram jerks his head towards the stairs.*)
Then call him. Quick.
(*He lets Coram go, pushing him to the stairs, where Coram half kneels on the steps.*)
CORAM Harry. Harry.
MILLIGAN Louder.
CORAM Harry.
(*A door opens upstairs. Faint music of a cracked gramophone.*)
HARRY (*heard from above*) What?
CORAM Harry?
HARRY Yes.
CORAM You've got company.
HARRY Never.
CORAM Harry.
HARRY (*off*) All right. All right.
(*A banging of doors and shuffling.*)
MILLIGAN I'll be over the street, right?
(*Coram nods. Milligan goes. Coram barely notices Harry coming down the stairs.*)
HARRY What d'you mean? Company?
CORAM Outside.

HARRY Eh?

CORAM Milligan.

HARRY Freddy Milligan?

CORAM Yes.

HARRY *(sitting on the stairs)* Oh.

CORAM He—he nearly punched a hole in my gut. *(Harry sighs)* He was fast,
Harry.

HARRY Aye.

CORAM Dead fast.

HARRY Aye. *(He allows a slight pause.)* 'Course, if you'd been properly
balanced up, like—

CORAM Aye. *(Harry sighs and makes as if to go.)* How old are you, Harry?

HARRY Sixty-seven. *(Showing his teeth.)* Bottom set's my own.

CORAM Aye.

HARRY *(turning as he remembers)* Hey.

CORAM What?

HARRY I forgot. *(Unwrapping them from a dreadful handkerchief.)* I got a
lovely set of uppers on the cart this morning. Lovely. Just the job
for you.

CORAM No.

HARRY They were given, you know. I mean, they didn't come from no
dustbin.

CORAM No.

HARRY I could have sold them.

CORAM It's just the idea. Something in my mouth. I don't fancy it.

HARRY Oh.

CORAM Don't take it that way.

HARRY What way?

CORAM Oh . . . *(He turns away. Harry makes it up.)*

HARRY Coram.

CORAM What?

HARRY I'm scared of him.

CORAM Milligan?

HARRY Aye.

CORAM You was in the house when he was born.

HARRY I was.

CORAM You're like an uncle to him.

HARRY Yes. Where is he?

CORAM Over the street.

HARRY Aye. He would be.
(He goes to the door to meet Milligan.)

The amusement arcade

(*Barlow is just taking aim. Ganger is watching.*)

BARLOW Oh, come on, Ganger. It's painful to look at you. (*He fires.*)

GANGER I've told you, Milligan used to work here, I thought he'd be useful for some breakin' and entering jobs but he wasn't. He's a panic merchant. I dismissed him.

BARLOW You've been filing these sights, haven't you?

GANGER Mr Barlow, don't be small-minded.

BARLOW He came back tonight.

GANGER Yes.

BARLOW You sent him away.

GANGER Yes.

BARLOW Where to?

GANGER I don't know. (*Barlow sighs.*) Have I ever told you a lie?

BARLOW No.

GANGER No. So I don't know where he is because I don't want to know. He's not what I'd call a man of the world.

BARLOW He's not what?

GANGER Well, he's no—no finesse. You know. No rubber gloves with him.

BARLOW You astound me.

GANGER Why? Milligan knows my business. So do you. He knows I won't help a catalogued man for four pound ten. You know I won't shop one for thirty five bob or whatever it is. Yet you're all in there, aren't you, calling me a hypocrite?

BARLOW You said it.

GANGER Your mind. I've read it.

BARLOW No you've not.

GANGER Eh?

BARLOW   Why *did* he come, eh?

GANGER   It's parole; it's inhuman.

BARLOW   That's why he panicked.

GANGER   I know.

BARLOW   It's not why he came here.

GANGER   Eh?

          (*The camera pans to a close-up of Barlow.*)

BARLOW   He came here, Ganger, because he knew you wouldn't help.

An alley opposite Coram's

(*The alley is on the opposite side of the road to Coram's. Milligan and Harry are just in the mouth of it.*)

MILLIGAN   Again, Harry, I mean again: wrong horse again. They just don't go for me. I mean. Tonight. Now. I could have got clear. I could have been in Lancaster now, or . . . but no, I trusted other people. All my life I've believed what people have said when they've had too many drinks or when—

HARRY   Hey.

MILLIGAN   People don't care, I mean, as you go through life you . . .

HARRY   You want to keep your belly full you know.

MILLIGAN   Who's ever loved me? My mother? No. She was sick of it by the time I came. My father? No.

HARRY   You can't run if you're strength's not up.

MILLIGAN   Margaret. Did she love me?

HARRY   I don't know.

MILLIGAN   No. And she's dead. That's my luck, eh? Pick a woman and she's dead at thirty-one.

HARRY   If you've nothing but halfpennies, suck beef cubes.

MILLIGAN   Eh?

HARRY   I'm giving you my experience.

MILLIGAN   Tell me where to kip.

HARRY   You can't kip now.

MILLIGAN   Why not?

HARRY   Well . . . they'll have dogs out.

MILLIGAN   No they—(*He hears a car, and looks quickly round.*) Get back.

HARRY   Eh?

MILLIGAN   Get back.

          (*He presses Harry back as the headlights flash over them. We hear the car halt.*)

HARRY   Freddy—

MILLIGAN   Shut up.

(*Cut to what Milligan sees: a mid-distant shot of Z Victor One halted outside Coram's. Jock and Fancy get out.*)

MILLIGAN Now come on, Harry. Quick.

HARRY I've given you fair warning. I said keep moving.

MILLIGAN Come on.

HARRY Keep moving.

MILLIGAN I'm tired. My head's splitting. I mean, you know me. You know my headaches.

HARRY Aye. I know 'em, but you got to keep moving.

Inside the lodging house

(*Jock and Fancy are standing in the empty hallway.*)

FANCY Come on. Where are you?

JOCK (*pulling the bell again*) There was someone at the upstairs window.

FANCY Aye. Come on.

CORAM (*heard from upstairs*) I'm full up.

FANCY You will be if you don't come down.

CORAM Eh?

(*He appears at the top of the stairs and starts to come down.*)
Oh, it's you.

FANCY Aye.

JOCK Does old Harry Smith still live here?

CORAM You know very well he does.

JOCK Can we see him?

CORAM He—er—he's just out for a minute.

FANCY We'll wait.

CORAM Suit yourself.

(*We cut to a shot from the previous position outside the door. Coram comes to close the door to as an excuse to look out to see if he can see what has happened to Harry.*)

JOCK I don't suppose you've had a visit from Freddy Milligan, have you?

CORAM Who?

FANCY You heard.

(*Cut back to shot from inside the door. Z Victor One is in the foreground. Behind we see Milligan running away.*
Coram comes away from the door and faces Fancy and Jock again.)

CORAM I told you, Mr Smith. Old Harry's just gone out, for the minute.

Newtown Police Station

(*Blackitt and Sweet are behind the desk. Alderman Wilson is still sitting waiting. There is a clock ticking kind of silence which the Alderman suddenly breaks.*)

WILSON   This—er—this man, sergeant.

BLACKITT   Er—I'm sorry, sir?

SWEET   (*to Blackitt, out of the side of the mouth*) Milligan.

BLACKITT   Eh?

WILSON   This man you're looking for: you know, the convict.

BLACKITT   Oh. Him.

WILSON   Pretty low type I suppose, is he? Eh?

BLACKITT   Well; you know, sir.

WILSON   I do. I know 'em inside out.
(*Blackitt and Sweet exchange a glance.*)
I mean, that's what I'm doing here, isn't it? When you know the enemy, you want to keep your own force up to the mark, don't you?
(*Cut to:*

A street

(*A brief tight shot of Milligan pausing, his breath coming hard and then falling over.*)

Inside the lodging house

(*Coram is sitting on the stairs. Fancy and Jock standing. Fancy sighs heavily with a meaningful glare at Coram.*)

CORAM   I told you; he—
(*He breaks off. We cut to what he has seen. Harry has arrived and is standing in the door.*)

FANCY   Hello, Harry.

HARRY   Evening.

FANCY   How's business?

HARRY   Slow. Springtime's the best for an handcart. When people chuck things out.

JOCK   We weren't thinking about rag-collecting.

HARRY   Oh?

CORAM   Freddy Milligan.

HARRY   Oh.
(*He thinks for a second and then jerks his head at Coram.*)
Has—er—has he said anything?

FANCY   No.

HARRY   Oh. (*He looks at Coram, with friendship and complicity.*)
'Course there being two of us, like, the money'd have to come up, wouldn't it?

CORAM   It would.

HARRY   Aye. Double money.

JOCK   Look, we don't know what you get. You'll have to sort that out
       with Mr Barlow.
HARRY He's a gentleman and all, isn't he?
FANCY Where's Milligan?
HARRY I gave him fair warning. Keep moving.
FANCY Where is he?
HARRY I sent him to the old railway station. You know.
FANCY Right.
       (*As Fancy and Jock go we cut to:*

Newtown Police Station

(*Blackitt is just snatching up a ringing phone. Sweet and Alderman
Wilson are still there.*)

BLACKITT (*to phone*) Right. Right you are. (*He puts the phone down.*) Sweet,
          Dog Van. Handlers. Whoever's in the canteen. Then telephone
          Mr Barlow at the Ganger's. (*He picks up another phone.*) Information
          Room. (*He sees Sweet is staring*) Come on lad. Milligan's at the old
          station.
          (*A close-up of Wilson before we cut to:*

A disused railway station

(*Milligan is just dropping down over a wall. He lands near the end of the
disused platform. He hears the whistle and distant noise of a train coming.
He has to decide. He runs towards the derelict waiting rooms. We see a
closer shot as Milligan tries the door, which is barred. He rips down a board
from a window. A flash shot of a hurtling train fills the picture.*)

Inside the Waiting Room

(*Milligan is on the sill. He leaps down into the derelict room just as the train passes. There is a roar and a flash of lights passing.*
In these lights, Whisky, a gaunt, tattered figure, rises screaming from the rubble on the floor.)

WHISKY Aaaaah . . .

(*Milligan lashes out. Whisky goes down. The lights abruptly stop. The noise recedes. Whisky is moaning slightly.*)

MILLIGAN (*shaken*) Don't you move.

WHISKY Whisky.

MILLIGAN Who are you?

WHISKY Whisky. Whisky.

MILLIGAN What d'you mean—?

(*He grabs Whisky, but lets him go in disgust.*) God, you're on the meths, aren't you? Eh?

WHISKY Whisky.

MILLIGAN You're on the meths. I've got the stink of you.

WHISKY No, no, no.

MILLIGAN Shut up.

WHISKY No. No. They got in. We put them out.

MILLIGAN Eh?

WHISKY I've got a bottle over there.

MILLIGAN I'm going.

WHISKY (*shouting*) No.

MILLIGAN Shut your gob. You'll have the whole world coming.

WHISKY Get my bottle.

MILLIGAN Eh?

WHISKY Bottle.

MILLIGAN Yes. Yes. Will you shut up?

WHISKY Cold. I'm cold all over.

MILLIGAN I'll find it.

WHISKY I'm cold. They got in the trench. Raiding party.

MILLIGAN Where is it?

WHISKY Eh?

MILLIGAN Your bottle.

WHISKY (*shivering violently*) Cold. Cold.

MILLIGAN All right.

WHISKY Cold.

(*Milligan sees the bottle and grabs it.*)

MILLIGAN Here. Now shut up.

(*He watches as Whisky takes the bottle and gulps. Holding it in two hands like an infant. It calms him down.*)

Right.

WHISKY (*moaning a little*) Oh . . . oh . . .

MILLIGAN I said you're right, aren't you?

WHISKY Don't go.

MILLIGAN I am going.

WHISKY No. No.

MILLIGAN Take your hands off.

WHISKY Story. Story. Might come again. All ranks.

MILLIGAN (*hitting him*) Off. Off.

WHISKY Face your front.

MILLIGAN I said—(*a final blow which knocks Whisky away*) take them off. You stink. You'll make me spew, you're—(*he breaks off as he realises that Whisky is crying.*) Look. Mate, I—I'm no good with this, you see, I—

WHISKY Story.

MILLIGAN I get headaches, you know, I—

WHISKY (*shouting*) Story.

MILLIGAN All right. But don't shout. You mustn't shout. You—you must be a good boy, you see, mate, and then I'll tell you the story. (*Whisky is shivering.*) Are you cold again? (*Whisky shakes his head.*) Gets you off like does it? A story?

WHISKY Story.

MILLIGAN Yes. Well, once upon a time there was a . . . (*He trails off. But Whisky is watching. Milligan gets up. Paces nervously.*) Once upon a time, there was a princess. No. A beautiful princess. At least I thought she was beautiful. I suppose I did anyway; and this princess, she lived in a big tall building, like and it was the way she looked, you see, her hair wasn't all rats-tails then, it was shining, and her—her—

her—well, in time of course she has a little princess of her own, as you might say . . . (*He puts his head out the other way.*)

(*Cut to shot out of window of policemen coming along line, and more police coming down the embankment over the lines.*)

MILLIGAN (*his voice continuing off the screen*) But they didn't live happily, you see. It wasn't nobody's fault, really, it was . . . It was just life I suppose you'd say. I mean, it was the way things were that were to blame. It wasn't the people, you see, the people was all . . . they're coming, mate. They've got dogs.

(*Cut back to the inside of the waiting room.*)

WHISKY Cold. I'm coming cold.

MILLIGAN They train 'em. Special. Bring a man down.

BARLOW (*calling from outside*) Milligan! Police!

WHISKY They're coming.

MILLIGAN Shut up.

WHISKY Your front. Face your front.

BARLOW Come on Freddy. Be sensible. You can't get clear.

MILLIGAN Shut up.

BARLOW Nitwit. We're coming in.

MILLIGAN (*to Whisky*) Your bottle.

WHISKY On the firestep. Every man.

MILLIGAN Where's your bottle?

(*Jock, with Fancy behind, appears on the window sill.*)

JOCK Hey. Come on now.

WHISKY Rapid fire . . .

(*Whisky crashes Jock down. Fancy is behind.*)

FANCY What the—?

WHISKY Aaaaah . . .

(*Fancy strikes him down. But is himself hit by Milligan, who needs the respite, and starts to scrabble.*)

MILLIGAN Your bottle. Where's your—? (*He takes it. He smashes off the end to make a deadly weapon. But Barlow is through the window.*)

BARLOW You won't need that Milligan.

(*Milligan turns and sees him.*)

BARLOW I'm surprised you picked it up, really.

MILLIGAN Come on then. Come on. All of you.

BARLOW No, no Freddy. You're going to drop it.

MILLIGAN No.

BARLOW I think so. You won't need it in cell, Freddy, and that's where you want to be isn't it? You're not running from Walton, Freddy. You're running from the hard, hard world.

MILLIGAN No.

BARLOW You got your fairy-tale ready of course; no money. People won't help. It gives you something to think about when you're in there, doesn't it? When you're all safe and cosy—

MILLIGAN No.

BARLOW When you're locked up and you've no worries.

MILLIGAN No.

BARLOW When you're locked up and you've no worries.

MILLIGAN No. (*But he has thrown down the bottle and slowly sinks to his knees.*)

BARLOW Don't worry Freddy. We'll soon have you back.

MILLIGAN No.

BARLOW They'll keep you safe. It'll be longer than six weeks.

MILLIGAN Margaret.

BARLOW Come on lad. My arm's stronger than yours.

MILLIGAN Margaret.
 (*Barlow looks at him.*)

MILLIGAN (*shouting*) Margaret. Who'll remember Margaret?
 (*A big close up of Milligan's weeping face, wretched and broken. Cut to the track outside, with a police dog alert.*)

The Police Station

GRAHAM Sergeant. They're here.

BLACKITT Right. Sweet. Tell the doctor. The meths. case.
 (*Smith, Weir and Whisky enter.*)

WILSON Excuse me. Is Mr Barlow—?

FANCY Yes, sir, he's just—
 (*Smith loses his grip on Whisky who falls down.*)

BLACKITT Look what you're doing, Smith.

JOCK	Come on you.
WHISKY	If you . . . if you . . .
FANCY	Get up.
WHISKY	If you want the whole battalion. I . . . I've . . .
	(*They take him out.*)
BLACKITT	I've seen them. I've seen them. Hanging on the old Barbed wire.
GRAHAM	Eh?
BLACKITT	You're too young.
	(*Barlow comes in.*)
BARLOW	Mr Wilson.
WILSON	Evening.
BARLOW	Sorry you had to wait, sir.
	(*Milligan has been brought in behind Barlow, who is blocking the way. Milligan is weeping. Barlow turns when he hears it and steps aside.*)
BARLOW	Well: get him in.
	(*They take Milligan out.*)
WILSON	Is that—?
BARLOW	Yes. That's him. (*To Blackitt*) I want Smith and Weir in my office.
BLACKITT	Yes, sir.
BARLOW	(*to Wilson*) After you, sir.
	(*Barlow and Wilson go into the C.I.D. office.*)
GRAHAM	What was that you said?
BLACKITT	Aye?
GRAHAM	About barbed wire.
BLACKITT	Nothing lad.
GRAHAM	Oh.
BLACKITT	Just be thankful it's not you that's meeting the Alderman, eh?
	(*The screen is filled by a shot of the outside of the prison.*)

A Place of Safety by John Hopkins

The Cast

Detective Chief Inspector Barlow
Detective Sergeant Watt
PC Jock Weir
PC Fancy Smith
Ann Fazakerly, on duty in the Information Room
Inspector Lowther, of the warrant department
Wallace, a warrant officer (who issues court orders)
Adigun Sadik, an immigrant from West Africa
Nana Sadik, his wife
A boy (also called Adigun) and a girl, their children
Mrs Lunt, caretaker of the tenement flats in which the Sadiks
　　lodge
Isaacs, an elderly jew who also lives there
Collins
Stephens

Also policemen, ambulance men, a crowd of drunken men,
　　children

A Place of Safety

Evening in a slum tenement in Seaport

(*We see a close shot of a pair of feet climbing stairs. They belong to Wallace, a heavily built man in his early fifties. He is wearing a light raincoat and a soft trilby hat. He is a warrant officer, on duty delivering court orders against people in debt. The filthy surroundings arouse no reaction in him at all. He is familiar with such tenement flats.*

When he reaches the landing, he stops for a moment, to glance at his wrist watch. He shrugs and walks on across the landing and up the stairs. Half a dozen children, negroes and Pakistanis, came running down the stairs towards him. Showing and laughing, they surge round him. One nearly bumps into Wallace, who puts him to one side, not unkindly, but completely indifferently.

The children run on down the stairs to the landing. The camera swings with them and holds them as they helter-skelter away, pushing past an old, fat Negress. who is plodding slowly up the stairs, carrying a heavy shopping bag. Her head is down and she is concentrating entirely on the effort it is to climb the stairs. The camera holds her on the screen whilst we hear Wallace, but do not see him. She doesn't look up when she hears Wallace knocking on Sadik's door.)

WALLACE (*Shouting out of vision*) Sadik!
(*The Negress walks slowly on. Wallace knocks on the door more violently.*)

WALLACE Come on, lad. You're in there. I know that.
(*The Negress reaches the landing and stops. She puts her shopping bag down and, supporting herself on the bannisters, she rests.*)

WALLACE (*very loudly, but still unseen*) Sadik!
(*She straightens up and reaches down to pick up the shopping bag, as Wallace bangs again on Sadik's door.*)

WALLACE It's only you suffers, keeping me stood here. D'you know that?
(*She trudges across the landing to the door of her room, which is at the bottom of the stairs leading up to Sadik's room.*)

WALLACE Sadik, I've come to take you . . .
(*She puts the bag down and takes a key out of her pocket.*)

WALLACE . . . and take you I bloody well will.
(*She puts the key into the lock of the door, as Wallace bangs on the door yet again. The knocking stops, and we hear Sadik's door scrape open out of vision.*)

WALLACE Aye, right—now . . .

(Wallace's voice stops suddenly, and he gives a rasping shout of pain. The camera tilts up sharply as Wallace staggers backwards to the top of the stairs and we now see him in the picture. He clutches his head with both hands, turns and pitches headlong down the stairs.

The camera zooms up to Sadik's expressionless face. We see him standing in the doorway of his room. He is holding a small hatchet in his hand. We hold him in close-up until, abruptly, he turns away.

Cut to:

Looking across the landing at Wallace, who is lying face down on the landing, his legs up the stairs behind him.

The door of the old Negress's room is shut and she has gone.

Slowly, lifting himself on to his elbows, and turning; Wallace tries to drag himself across the landing.

The door of Sadik's room slams shut.)

Inside Sadik's room

(Sadik drags the bed across the room and bangs it hard against the door. The bed is an old, iron one. It is covered with a clean, candlewick cover. The room is scrupulously clean. The walls are hung with coloured blankets as decoration, but underneath the paint is old, and the wallpaper in tatters. Sadik straightens up and looks round. His wife, Nana, is standing by the fireplace, watching him. She is twenty-five, a half-caste Indian. We cut to Sadik looking at her across the room. He drops the hatchet on to the floor, and sits on the bed. He is twenty-eight, a Negro, not very tall and slightly built.

A little girl crawls out of a cupboard and scurries across to Nana. She crouches at her feet.

There is a pause.

A boy looks round the back of a chair in the corner of the room, and then runs to Nana. He crouches beside the little girl on the floor at Nana's feet. We cut to Sadik as he stands up, walks across to a chair and picks it up bodily. He turns and throws it across the bed against the door.)

The staircase

(Wallace is crawling across the landing to the top of the stairs. The camera is looking over his shoulder as he looks down the precipitous flight and tries to lever himself up on to his feet. One hand on the bannisters, the other against the floor, he pushes and pulls. At the last moment, almost on to his knees, he loses his balance and falls forward, down the stairs.)

The hall downstairs

(Mrs Lunt is standing in the doorway of her room at the end of the hall, which is out of sight of the foot of the stairs.

Mrs Lunt is sixty-five. She is a widow and she is clinging to her job as caretaker, watchdog for the landlord. She listens to the sound of Wallace falling down the stairs.

There is a pause.)

MRS LUNT *(shouting)* What you doing up there? *(Pause)* Eh!

(She gets no reply, so she walks out into the hall. She stops and checks to see she has a key in the pocket of her apron. She hasn't. She turns and walks back into her room.

Another pause.

She comes out again, carrying the key and pulls the door shut behind her. Then she pushes it to make certain it is securely shut.

The camera pulls back with her as she walks forward and swings as she turns the corner at the bottom of the stairs. It tilts up with her, as she starts to walk up the stairs.

Wallace is kneeling at the top of the flight of stairs, clinging to the bannisters. The camera zooms up to him.)

The street outside

(Looking down from the top floor of a house in the street at the corner, as Z Victor One turns into the street. We can just glimpse the solid line of similar slum tenements on either side of the street.

The camera swings with it as it drives along and then stops at the pavement.

Fancy Smith gets out of the car and walks quickly across the pavement, up

157

the steps to the front door, which is standing open, and straight into the house.)

The hall of the tenement

(Looking up the flight of stairs. Wallace is lying across the top of the stairs, on his face, unconscious. We see him, but only hear Mrs Lunt.)

MRS LUNT Up there he is.

FANCY *(also unseen, coldly)* I can see him.
(He walks past the camera and away up the stairs towards Wallace.)

Inside Z Victor One

(The car is parked, and Jock is speaking into the radio.)

JOCK Off-watch—28 Ashmore Street. *(He looks up as he hears the sound of an ambulance bell.)*

ANN *(heard over the car radio)* Roger Z Victor One.

JOCK The ambulance is here.

The landing of the staircase

(The ambulance bell clangs loudly outside the house. Inside the house, silence. Fancy eases Wallace over on to his back.)

MRS LUNT *(heard from below)* Is he—like—dead? Is he?
(Fancy takes off his cap and bends over Wallace, to listen to his heart.)

FANCY Where's the fellow did this?

MRS LUNT Don't know.
(Fancy lifts his head fractionally, to look down the stairs at Mrs Lunt.)

FANCY *(quietly)* You don't know!

MRS LUNT I was in my room. How should I know?
(Unseen, Jock has entered the front door, and now calls up the stairs.)

JOCK Hey, Fancy.

The hall at the foot of the stairs

(Jock is standing beside Mrs Lunt at the bottom of the stairs, looking up at Fancy.)

JOCK How's he doing?

FANCY He's alive.

JOCK The ambulance is here.

FANCY I heard it.
(Jock puts a hand on Mrs Lunt's shoulder.)

JOCK Look—d'you mind?

MRS LUNT What's that?

JOCK Give us a bit of room—eh?

(The ambulance men walk into the hall.)

FANCY He's up here.

(The ambulance men put the stretcher against the wall and walk up the stairs.)

JOCK What happened?

MRS LUNT I don't know.

JOCK Fight?

MRS LUNT I don't know.

JOCK Who is he?

MRS LUNT *(irritably)* I don't know.

JOCK *(coldly)* Does he live here?

MRS LUNT Don't be daft!

JOCK What d'you say!

MRS LUNT *(grumbling)* Well, look at him—is it likely?

JOCK Have you?

MRS LUNT What?

JOCK Had a look at him?

MRS LUNT No.

JOCK What d'you mean then?

MRS LUNT White, in't he? You can see he's white.

JOCK Oh.

MRS LUNT Would he live in a place like this? Would he?

JOCK Calling on someone?

MRS LUNT Maybe so.

(The two ambulance men carry Wallace down the stairs and lay him on the floor.)

JOCK Who?

MRS LUNT I don't know.

JOCK Did you see him come in?

MRS LUNT No.

JOCK Didn't speak to him?

(The ambulance men put the stretcher beside Wallace.)

MRS LUNT If I didn't see him . . .

JOCK He didn't ask you—maybe—where does some bloke live? Some bloke he wanted to see?

MRS LUNT I didn't see him come in. I didn't talk to him.

FANCY *(heard shouting further up the stairs)* Where are you then?

The landing

(Fancy is standing on the landing.)

FANCY *(loudly)* All of you!

Inside Sadik's room

(*Sadik is standing with his back to the window, listening, but motionless.*)

FANCY (*heard from below*) Where're you hiding?

(*There is a silent pause, while Sadik remains still.*)

The landing

(*A door opens and a man looks out, a young Negro.*)

FANCY There's a fellow been half-killed, d'you know? (*The man shakes his head.*)

Here. (*He points at the floor.*) Like—just here. Can you see the blood?

(*The man looks at the floor, where Fancy is pointing and then, looks up at Fancy again.*)

FANCY Did you hear anything? (*The man shakes his head.*) See nothing? (*The man shakes his head. A door across the landing opens and an old man looks out, another Negro.*)

FANCY What about you, dad? (*Pause*) Heard nothing? Saw nothing? (*Pause*) Ah! Get back in your holes, why don't you!

JOCK What's the matter with you?

(*Jock walks up on to the landing.*)

FANCY Look at them! (*He points at the watching faces.*) Sat right in there and they know nothing. Saw nothing!

JOCK Maybe they didn't.

FANCY Heard something. Must've heard something! He was lying there— fell from up there. (*He points up the stairs.*) D'you see?

JOCK Oh, aye.

(*Jock walks across the landing and looks up the stairs.*)

FANCY Must hear a bloke like that, falling down a flight of stairs.

JOCK You'd think so.

FANCY (*turning on the old man*) You must!

JOCK (*looking round at the old man*) You heard nothing?

(*The old man shakes his head.*)

FANCY You're deaf, are you? Deaf, is that it? Deaf!

JOCK Leave him alone, Fancy.

FANCY You know who it was, do you?

JOCK What?

FANCY With his head split open—d'you know who it was?

JOCK No.

FANCY Tom Wallace.

JOCK Wallace?

FANCY From the court—warrant officer.

JOCK Oh!

FANCY Likely come to serve a warrant—on someone.
(*He looks across the landing at the young Negro.*) D'you reckon?

JOCK I'll check with Headquarters. (*He walks to the top of the stairs.*)

FANCY Hey! How many ways out of here?

JOCK Just the front door?

FANCY No back way?

JOCK There's a door into the coal yard at the back.

FANCY Aye, well—one of us better . . .

JOCK You have to go through the old woman's room to get to it.

FANCY Oh. Right, I'll have a look upstairs.
(*Jock starts to walk down the stairs as we cut back to:*

The hall

(*Looking through a half-open doorway, over the shoulder of a young Negress, out into the hall, watching Jock as he walks down the stairs. He stops at the bottom of the stairs and glances at the doorway. The door shuts quickly.*)

The hall

(*We have cut to a view from the front door, showing Jock looking back along the hall at Mrs Lunt, who is standing in the doorway of her room.*)

JOCK Anyone comes that way—wants to go out the back—give us a shout.

MRS LUNT I'll shout.

JOCK Aye. (*He turns and walks away along the hall.*)

Outside in the street

(*Looking down into the street as Jock walks out of the house, down the steps and opens the door of Z Victor One.*)

The Information Room at H.Q.

ANN Roger, Z Victor One.

Inspector Lowther's office

(*The telephone on the desk rings. Lowther takes his cap off again and walks back to his desk. He puts the cap down and picks the receiver up.*)

LOWTHER Inspector Lowther, warrant department . . . Oh, yes. What can I do for you? . . . Wallace? Yes? What about him? . . . Injured? How d'you mean—injured? . . . For God's sake! What happened? . . . Yes . . . Just a minute. (*He puts down the receiver and walks across his office to the door. He opens the door and looks out briefly. He turns and walks back to his desk and picks up the receiver again.)* Hallo? . . . Look, my secretary's gone for the day. But if you can tell me exactly what information you want? *(He picks up a biro from a pen stand.)* Yes—er—just . . . *(Lowther walks round his desk and opens the elaborate blotter he keeps in the centre of it.)* Let me write that down. 28, Ashmore Street, Seaport. Yes, I've got that. *(He straightens up again.)* Assuming he was there serving a warrant on someone, you'd like to know who it was.

Inside Z Victor One

ANN *(heard over the car radio)* Wallace was serving a warrant for committal on Adigun Sadik.

(Jock is writing with his note-book balanced on his knee.)

JOCK *(carefully)* Sadik.

ANN Yes, Z Victor One. That is spelt S A D I K.

The landing outside Sadik's room

(Fancy is standing at the top of the stairs, looking down.)

FANCY *(shouting)* Hey, missis.

(There is a pause.)

Missis.

MRS LUNT *(from below)* What d'you want?

FANCY Come up here.

MRS LUNT Do what?

FANCY I said . . . *(He takes a step down onto the stairs and leans over the ban-*

nisters.) Come up here.

MRS LUNT I can't.

FANCY (*quietly*) By heck.

The hall of the tenement

(*We see Mrs Lunt glaring up the stairs, and hear Fancy from above.*)

MRS LUNT Climb all them stairs? Get off.

FANCY I'm not coming down.

MRS LUNT You'll have to lump it then, won't you?

The landing outside Sadik's room

FANCY (*shouting down*) Who is it lives up here, Missis? The top room?

MRS LUNT (*from below*) What d'you say?

Inside Sadik's room

(*Sadik is crouched by the bed. Nana is standing by the fireplace, with the two children at her feet.*)

FANCY (*heard from outside the door*) Is there someone lives up here? In the top room?

The hall below

MRS LUNT A blackie. Name of Sadik—or some such nonsense.

JOCK That's him. (*He walks past Mrs Lunt, starts to walk up the stairs, and calls up.*) Fancy!

The landing outside Sadik's room

FANCY What?

JOCK (*from below*) Hang on. I'm coming up.

Inside Sadik's room

(*Sadik turns his head and looks across the room at Nana.*)

FANCY (*from outside*) Buck up then.

(*Sadik picks up the hatchet and puts it down on the bed in front of him. There is knocking on the door.*)

FANCY Hey—Sadik—whatever your name is. Are you in there?

(*Nana takes the girl across to the cupboard and opens it. The girl goes inside and Nana shuts the door.*)

FANCY Are you?

(*Fancy bangs on the door again. The boy scuttles across the room and hides behind the chair.*)

JOCK (*heard as he is mounting the stairs*) Fancy.

The landing outside Sadik's room

FANCY What?

(*Jock walks up the last steps to the landing.*)

JOCK (*quietly*) This is the bloke.

FANCY (*nodding at the door of Sadik's room.*) What?

JOCK Wallace was here to knock him off.

FANCY Thought so.

JOCK You what!

FANCY Here. (*He points to a place on the wall.*) There's that much filth on the walls, you can't hardly see.

JOCK What?

FANCY Blood.

(*Jock leans forward.*)

FANCY (*grinning*) Don't get too close. They can jump.

JOCK (*quietly*) Looks like blood.

FANCY Took his fall from here, I reckon. Tried to save himself.

(*Jock stands at the top of the stairs, looking down.*)

FANCY You can see. Caught at the bannisters.

JOCK Oh, aye.

FANCY More blood. (*He leans on the bannisters.*) There's an old woman lives there. (*He points down the stairs.*) Right at the bottom—d'you see?

JOCK What about her?

FANCY Heard nothing. Saw nothing. Couldn't hardly see me—and I was stood right in front of her.

(Jock turns and looks across the landing at the door.)

JOCK Is he in there?

FANCY I give him a shout.

(Jock walks across to the door.)

FANCY If he's in there, he's not letting on.

JOCK Sadik. Are you in there?

FANCY 'Course, he maybe doesn't understand.

JOCK What?

FANCY English. Like—doesn't speak the lingo. *(He walks across the landing door and bangs on the door.)* Hey. Come on, lad. Don't mess us about.

Inside Sadik's room

(Sadik is crouched in the middle of the room, the hatchet gripped in his hand.

Nana is standing by the fireplace watching him.)

The landing outside Sadik's room

(Fancy tries the handle of the door. It turns. He looks at Jock and then, he puts some pressure on the door and pushes against it. The door moves, but only slightly. Then it jams.)

Inside Sadik's room

(Sadik brings the hatchet up and clutches it against his chest.)

165

The landing outside Sadik's room

FANCY (*quietly*) He's in there. (*He looks across the door at Jock.*) Something holding the door shut.
(*Fancy brings his shoulder away from the door and prepares to break the door in.*)

JOCK (*quietly*) Hey. (*He beckons Fancy away from the door.*)

FANCY What d'you want?
(*Jock and Fancy stand at the top of the stairs, talking quietly.*)

JOCK I just thought—you know we haven't a lot of cause.

FANCY What.

JOCK Pushing in there.

FANCY Cause?

JOCK We don't know it was him clobbered Wallace.

FANCY Fair idea.

JOCK Oh, aye—maybe so.

FANCY And one thing's certain. We'll get no further with him in there and us stuck out here.

JOCK We don't even know he's in there.

MRS LUNT (*yelling from below*) He's in there.

FANCY Is he?
(*Mrs Lunt is now standing on the lower landing.*)

MRS LUNT I saw him come in.

FANCY Thanks.

MRS LUNT What d'you reckon? Has he gone beserk? Has he?

FANCY Thought you couldn't get up here?

MRS LUNT 'Course, if he has—you'll need to look out for yourselves. won't you? If he's gone beserk.

FANCY   Aye. (*He turns away and looks at the door.*)
MRS LUNT   And he's got his wife, in there, you know—and his kids.
JOCK   Has he?
MRS LUNT   I read where one of them blackies did his whole family in.
JOCK   Wife and kids?
MRS LUNT   Whole family.
JOCK   (*irritably*) Sadik?
MRS LUNT   What?
JOCK   He's got his wife and kids in there?
MRS LUNT   I don't know where else they'd be.
(*Jock and Fancy walk back to the door of Sadik's room.*)
FANCY   What d'you reckon he's got?
JOCK   Knife—maybe—an axe.
FANCY   He made a bloody mess of old Wallace.
JOCK   Took him by surprise.
FANCY   Hmm.
(*Jock knocks on the door again.*)
JOCK   Sadik? (*There is a slight pause.*) Are you in there, Sadik?
MRS LUNT   (*calling*) He's in there. I told you.
FANCY   (*turning away from the door*) Look, you . . .
(*As Fancy turns away we cut to a close-up of the frightened Sadik.*)

Inside Sadik's room

(*Close-up of Sadik, sweat streaming down his face.*

We can hear, muffled by the closed door, the girl sobbing in the cupboard.)
FANCY   (*heard from outside the door*) . . . shut up.

MRS LUNT (*also heard from outside*) You've no call talking to me like that.
FANCY Get off downstairs.
MRS LUNT I'm caretaker here. I've every right . . .
FANCY Shall I carry on?

The landing outside Sadik's room

(*We see a close-up of Mrs Lunt as we hear the irritated Fancy.*)
FANCY (*out of sight*) Like—over my shoulder?
MRS LUNT (*rumbling*) You've no call . . . (*she turns away*) talking like that.
(*We cut to Jock, who is standing by Sadik's door.*)
JOCK (*abruptly*) Fancy.
FANCY Well.
JOCK Come here.
FANCY Gets on your wick.
JOCK I can hear something.
FANCY What?
JOCK I don't know. (*Pause*) There's someone in there.
FANCY Right. (*He stands squarely in front of the door.*) I'll kick it. You catch me.
JOCK Both in together?
FANCY Aye. (*He steadies himself.*) Could do with a bit of help, couldn't we?
JOCK It's crying—somebody crying.
(*Fancy swings his leg up and kicks the door at the lock, as we cut to:*

The hall downstairs

(*Barlow and Watt have just come in.*)
BARLOW (*sharply*) What's that? (*He turns and looks up the stairs.*) What the devil . . . ?
WATT Smith and Weir . . .
BARLOW What?
WATT Should be about somewhere.
BARLOW What are they doing? (*He calls up the stairs to Mrs Lunt, who is walking slowly down.*) What's going on up there?
MRS LUNT I don't know.
BARLOW (*shouting up the stairs*) Smith! Weir!

The landing outside Sadik's room

(*The door has not opened. Jock is standing beside it against the wall. Fancy is standing in front of the door, looking at it venomously.*)
BARLOW (*heard from below*) What're you doing up there, Smith?

168

FANCY   (*to Jock*) D'you notice? It's always me he goes for.
        (*Fancy grins and turns away from the door.*)
BARLOW   (*shouting*) Smith!
        (*Fancy leans over the bannisters.*)
FANCY   Sir?

The landing halfway down

(*We are looking at the young negro and, standing at his shoulder, his young wife, who are standing in the doorway. As they look out to see what the noise is about, we hear the instructions shouted by Barlow below.*)

BARLOW   Whatever you're doing, Smith—stop.
FANCY   (*heard from above*) Sir?
BARLOW   D'you understand?
FANCY   Yes, sir.
BARLOW   Right.
FANCY   Shall we come down, sir?
BARLOW   What?
FANCY   I said . . .
BARLOW   No. Stay where you are.
FANCY   Sir.
BARLOW   And do nothing.

The hall below

(*Barlow, Watt, and a group of uniformed men have squeezed in. Barlow turns and looks at Watt.*)

BARLOW   Have a look round the back.

WATT Yes, sir.

(*Barlow looks at Mrs Lunt, who is now standing at the bottom of the stairs, blocked by the assembled policemen.*)

BARLOW Who're you?

MRS LUNT Who are you?

BARLOW Detective Chief Inspector Barlow.

MRS LUNT Oh. Well, I'm the caretaker here, Mrs Lunt.

BARLOW Right, what's the quickest way round to the back.

MRS LUNT Out the front door—turn right . . .

BARLOW No back door?

MRS LUNT (*reluctantly*) Well, yes—there is.

BARLOW Where?

MRS LUNT Through there.

(*She points along the hall to the door of her room.*)

BARLOW Show Sergeant Watt.

MRS LUNT That's *my* room.

BARLOW He'll keep his eyes shut. (*To Watt*) See what you can find.

WATT Yes, sir.

MRS LUNT Can I get by then?

BARLOW What?

MRS LUNT Make a bit of room.

BARLOW Oh yes.

(*Barlow gestures the men away from the bottom of the stairs. Mrs Lunt turns the corner at the bottom of the stairs.*)

BARLOW You know this bloke, do you?

MRS LUNT Eh?

BARLOW Sadik. You know him?

MRS LUNT (*reluctantly*) Yes.

BARLOW Right-handed? Left-handed?

MRS LUNT You what?

BARLOW (*calmly*) Is he right-handed or is he left-handed?

MRS LUNT I don't know.

BARLOW (*in close-up*) Think.

MRS LUNT I've never noticed never bothered . . .

BARLOW Take his rent, do you?

MRS LUNT Yes.

BARLOW All right.

(*There is a pause.*)

MRS LUNT Look, it's daft. I don't know if he's . . .

BARLOW (*harshly*) Bloody think!

(*Involuntarily everyone shifts a little distance away from Barlow. There is another pause.*)

MRS LUNT (*quietly*) Right-handed.

BARLOW Thank you Mrs Lunt. That saves a lot of trouble—maybe saves someone's life.

WATT Er—Mr Barlow?

BARLOW Yes, John?

WATT Shall we get everyone out of the house?

BARLOW I don't think so. Not yet, anyway. See how it goes. (*He glances across the hall at an open door to one of the tenants' rooms. It is shut from inside.*) No need to tell them to keep out of the way.

MRS LUNT Are you coming? (*She is standing in the open doorway of her room.*)

BARLOW You, and you . . . (*he points at two of the constables*) stay down here. You two—the first landing. *The two constables indicated, start to walk up the stairs.*) You and you—come with me. (*To Watt*) Go on, John—the lady's getting impatient.

(*Watt turns and walks away along the hall.*)

The landing outside Sadik's room

(*Fancy is leaning on the bannisters. Jock is standing at the top of the stairs looking down. They are listening to the men walking up the uncarpeted stairs.*)

JOCK (*grinning*) Charge of the Light Brigade.

FANCY Errol Flynn and all, d'you reckon?

JOCK Who needs Errol Flynn!

(*We hear a heavy object scraped across the floor in Sadik's room. Jock and Fancy turn instantly to face the door of the room, alert. We cut to:*

Inside Sadik's room

(*Sadik is struggling with the bed, pulling it away from the door. As soon as there is sufficient room for him to get between the door and the bed, he runs round the end of the bed and throws his body against the door, slamming it.*)

The landing outside Sadik's room

(*Jock and Fancy are watching the door intently.*)

BARLOW (*quietly from just below*) You two. Come down here. (*Pause*) Smith. Weir.

(*Jock and Fancy turn and walk across the landing. Cut to Barlow looking up the stairs at them, as they walk down.*)

BARLOW What're you at? Hmm? (*Fancy reaches the landing first.*)

FANCY Sir?

BARLOW What d'you think you're doing?

JOCK   He's in there, sir. (*He steps on to the landing, beside Fancy.*)

BARLOW   I know he's in there, Weir. I was asking what you thought you were doing.

JOCK   We were trying to get him out.

BARLOW   (*brightly*) You haven't?

JOCK   No, sir.

BARLOW   No. What've you tried? No—don't tell me. Brute force and a load of ignorance. Like—kick the door down!

FANCY   He won't walk out.

BARLOW   Won't he? (*Pause*) Tried to persuade him, have you?

FANCY   Yes, sir.

BARLOW   (*mimicking a tough approach*) 'Come out—or I'll smash your face in'?

JOCK   I tried to get him to talk.

BARLOW   What was your mate doing? Kicking the door down?

FANCY   (*bitterly*) If he's the bloke clobbered Tom Wallace . . . .

BARLOW   He is. Oh, yes—didn't you know that?

JOCK   Pretty certain.

BARLOW   If it wasn't . . .

JOCK   It was him Wallace came to see.

BARLOW   Right couple of idiots you'd have looked! Door off it's hinges. Him clobbered. All 'cause you . . . (*He stops and looks at Jock and Fancy for a moment.*) Ah! (*He breaks off, disgusted. He turns to the two constables with him.*) I want you two stood—one on either side of the door. Off you go. (*As the two constables move forward.*) Quietly. (*The two constables walk away up the stairs, towards the door of Sadik's room.*)

Inside Sadik's room

(*Sadik is standing with his back against the wall, immediately beside the door, listening to the slight shuffling noises on the landing outside.*)

The landing outside Sadik's room

(*Barlow is standing just at the bottom of the half flight of stairs, talking to Jock and Fancy.*)

BARLOW   According to the old woman downstairs, he's right-handed. Don't bank on that—she could be wrong—just—favour that side, when he comes out.

(*Jock and Fancy start to walk up the stairs. Barlow stops them.*)

Look—he had just the one go at Wallace; likely fractured his skull —and cut off most of one ear. Watch him.

(Barlow walks away up the stairs and takes up a position facing Sadik's door, with his back against the bannisters. He gestures Jock past him to stand on the right-hand side of the door, and gestures Fancy to stay on the left-hand side. As they settle into their positions, he puts out both arms in a gesture commanding absolute silence.
There is a pause.
Barlow lets his arms drop and relax at his side.)

BARLOW *(calmly)* Mr Sadik.

Inside Sadik's room

(We see a close-up of Sadik, standing back against the wall listening to Barlow.)

BARLOW *(heard from outside the door)* I want you to listen to what I'm going to say, I want you to listen very carefully.

The landing outside Sadik's room

(We see Barlow again as he speaks deliberately.)

BARLOW My name is Barlow. I'm a Detective Chief Inspector. Now, I've come up here to talk to you, to tell you exactly how things stand. Then I'm going to offer you some advice. I hope you'll take it, Mr Sadik, because I think it's good advice.

Inside Sadik's room

(We are looking across the room holding Sadik at the door with the hatchet in his hand, and Nana standing by the fireplace, watching him.)

BARLOW (*heard from outside*) I wouldn't—normally, I wouldn't take all this trouble—but I think, in this case—well, I think you need help.

The landing outside Sadik's room

(*We are looking along the landing, holding Barlow standing back against the bannisters, and the constables, standing by the door.*)

BARLOW I think you deserve help. (*Pause*) I'll tell you what I've done, Mr Sadik. I've sent all my men away. They're waiting downstairs. I brought a lot of men with me. I expect you understand, I had to. Now I've sent them all away, so I can talk to you.

(*Jock turns his head and looks across the landing at Barlow. Abruptly, angrily, Barlow brings up a hand and points at the door. Jock quickly looks away.*)

BARLOW I've heard the facts of the case. I know you hit this man Wallace. Hit him—and he fell down these stairs. I think I ought to explain, Mr Sadik—however the injuries were caused, whether by the blow, or by the fall . . .

Inside Sadik's room

(*We see the silent Nana in close-up.*)

BARLOW (*heard from outside*) . . . you are still responsible in law. So—first, the situation is serious. I'm not going to pretend it isn't. I'm not going to lie to you. I've spoken to Wallace and I've spoken to his doctors. He has a fractured skull.

The landing outside Sadik's room

BARLOW That's serious. But it isn't fatal. He has identified you as the person who attacked him. I don't imagine you're going to deny it.

Inside Sadik's room

(*We see a close-up of Sadik.*)

BARLOW (*heard from outside*) So, I've come here to find out your side of things. I want to know why you did it. You're not mad, so you must have a reason.

The landing outside Sadik's room

BARLOW I want to know what it is. I hope you're going to tell me. Talk to me, at least. That's why I've come here.

Inside Sadik's room

(*We see a close-up of Sadik's hands at the lock.*)

BARLOW (*heard from outside*) Mr Sadik? (*Pause*) It's in your hands now. I've done—as much as I can. Now . . .

The landing outside Sadik's room

(*The camera shows a close-up of the door handle.*)

BARLOW . . . it's up to you. (*There is a pause. The handle remains still. Barlow continues coldly.*) Then I'm afraid there's nothing more I can do. (*The door handle turns.*)

Inside Sadik's room

(*Sadik has changed the hatchet into his left hand, in order to turn the handle of the door.*

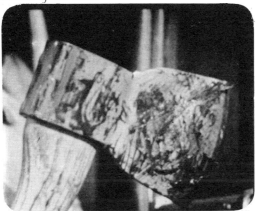

Nana steps urgently away from the fireplace. The camera moves quickly across the room towards her.)

NANA (*desperately*) No!

(*But Sadik starts to open the door. We see Barlow over Sadik's shoulder. Sadik steps into the doorway. He looks directly across the landing at Barlow, who smiles. Sadik steps on to the landing.*)

BARLOW The left hand.

The landing outside Sadik's room

(*Jock and the constable on Sadik's left side catch hold of his arm and wrist. He jerks round to face them, as Fancy and the other constable catch hold of his other arm. They stretch his arms and wrestle for the hatchet, which swings dangerously.*

Barlow steps across and catches hold of the wrist as it swings down. He jerks it hard. Sadik shouts with pain and lets go of the hatchet.)

BARLOW   Mind your feet!

(*The hatchet falls to the floor. Sadik struggles and twists to break free from the four constables.*)

BARLOW   Don't play games with him!

(*The constable on the right side snaps on the handcuffs to Sadik's wrist and then on to his own. Fancy gets round behind Sadik and holds him in a bear hug as the other constable snaps hand-cuffs on to his left wrist and then on to his own.*)

BARLOW   Take him down to the car.

(*The two constables lead Sadik, who is momentarily passive, staring at Barlow, to the stairs and start to take him down. Barlow bends down and picks up the hatchet.*)

BARLOW   I said, didn't I? Don't bank on it.

JOCK   Yes, sir.

BARLOW   (*Handing the hatchet to Fancy*) You can look after that, Smith.

FANCY   Sir.

(*Jock and Fancy turn towards the top of the stairs.*)

BARLOW   Did you notice anything, Smith?

FANCY   Sir?

BARLOW   About him?

FANCY   He was left-handed?

BARLOW   He walked out.

FANCY   Oh. Yes, sir—he did.

BARLOW   Treat them like animals, you get animals to deal with. (*He steps into the doorway of Sadik's room.*) Treat them like normal human beings, they won't know what you're talking about, but you've more chance—getting them to do what they're told.

The landing halfway down the stairs

(*Gathering his strength, Sadik suddenly sweeps the constable on his right off-balance, and throws him side-ways against the wall. The constable on his left jerks hard on the hand-cuff and wrenches Sadik, still struggling, towards him. The two constables standing on the landing join in and one of them catches Sadik round the throat. Sadik gives a half-strangled cry and lurches forward on to his knees. His head goes down and he stops struggling.*)

The landing outside Sadik's room

(*Barlow is standing in the doorway of Sadik's room. Fancy is standing at the top of the stairs, and Jock a few steps down.*)

BARLOW You'd better go down. Sounds like they need some help.
(*Barlow turns and walks through into Sadik's room.*)

Inside Sadik's room

BARLOW Mrs Sadik?
NANA Yes.
BARLOW You're all right?
NANA Yes.
(*Barlow looks at the room casually as he closes the door.*)
BARLOW I was told you've children?
NANA Yes.
BARLOW They're here?
NANA (*calling quietly*) Adigun.
(*The boy scrambles out from behind the chair and runs to Nana.*)
BARLOW Well, I can see he hasn't come to very much harm.
NANA (*unresponsively*) No. (*She walks across to the cupboard and opens it. The girl crawls out.*) They have come to no harm.
BARLOW Good.
(*The girl stands beside Nana.*)
(*There is a shout from outside. Nana crosses to the window and looks out.*)

The street outside

(*The camera is looking down at the pavement outside the house, where Z Victor One is pulled up. Sadik is bundled out of the front door. The constables on either side of him hold his arms tight with their free hands. Jock and Fancy follow them. Jock walks round the trio, down the steps to the car and*) *opens the back door. The constables bring Sadik forward. He sees the car, the open door, the uniform standing beside it, and starts to struggle again. Fancy steps up behind and grips his shoulders. The three constables hustle him towards the car and he starts to kick out with his legs, to shout.*

The street is silent around the struggling men. They bend Sadik over and the three linked men scramble into the car. Fancy slams the door.)

Inside Sadik's room

NANA   I knew you would trick him!

BARLOW   *(briskly)* If you can make arrangements for the children Mrs Sadik—perhaps they can stay with a friend? I'd like you to come to the police station.

NANA   No.

BARLOW   *(abruptly)* It's possible you can help your husband . . .

NANA   I cannot leave them.

BARLOW   Oh.

NANA   But I will come.

Inside Z Victor One

(Sadik is in the middle on the back seat, his arms stretched across the constables sitting on either side of him. His head is down on his chest and he is sobbing.)

The hall of the tenement

(Isaacs, an amiable Jew, in his middle sixties, is standing in the hall, talking to Mrs Lunt.)

MRS LUNT The blackie! They've just now took him off.

ISAACS I know, I know. Didn't I see?

MRS LUNT What're you doing then? Asking can you talk to him?

ISAACS To him—I am not asking. To his wife—maybe—to the police.

MRS LUNT Plenty of them.

ISAACS They are still here?

MRS LUNT Ha!

ISAACS I see them leave with Mr Sadik. I see others leave . . .

MRS LUNT Plenty more where they came from. Half a dozen out the back still, far as I know.

ISAACS To them I wish to speak.

MRS LUNT You're welcome.

ISAACS Where will I find them?

MRS LUNT Wait here I should. They're all over the house. I should just wait here—catch them on the way out.

ISAACS Thank you.
(There is a pause and we see Mrs Lunt in medium close-up.)

MRS LUNT What're you going to tell them?

ISAACS *(shrugging)* If you don't mind.

MRS LUNT Something about him, is it?
(Barlow walks down the stairs, followed by Nana, and the children.)
Something about the blackie?

ISAACS *(Gesturing at Barlow.)* Is this—perhaps . . .

MRS LUNT What? Ye—oh, yes—that's one of them.

ISAACS *(to Barlow)* Excuse me.

BARLOW Yes. *(He stops at the bottom of the stairs.)* What is it?

ISAACS Can I speak to you?

BARLOW	What about?
ISAACS	This unfortunate—er—no—terrible business!
BARLOW	Who're you?
ISAACS	My name is Isaacs.
BARLOW	You live here?
ISAACS	No. Oh, no. I live across the street. Number twenty.
BARLOW	I see. (*Pause*) Well?
ISAACS	Er . . . I should prefer . . .

(*Isaacs shrugs and glances at Mrs Lunt. Barlow looks at Mrs Lunt.*)

BARLOW	Yes, so would I. Tell you what, Isaacs—you know the police station?
ISAACS	Yes. Oh yes—of course.
BARLOW	Come along and talk to me there. Chief Inspector Barlow.
ISAACS	Oh.
BARLOW	I'd give you a lift—only . . . (*he glances back at Nana and the children*) . . . I've a lorry-full already.
ISAACS	No. No, of course.
BARLOW	I'll be working late.
ISAACS	(*quietly*) Hmm.
BARLOW	If you've something to tell me . . .
ISAACS	(*firmly*) I will see you there.
BARLOW	Right. Come along Mrs Sadik.

(*Barlow walks away to the front door. Nana and the children follow him. They all go out.*)

MRS LUNT	(*eagerly*) 'Bout the blackie, is it?
ISAACS	The police station.
MRS LUNT	Know something, do you?
ISAACS	What?
MRS LUNT	Do you?
ISSACS	I have to go to the police station.

(*There is slight pause.*)

MRS LUNT	Likely lock you away. Set foot in there. That's what they'll do. You go speaking up for blackies—likely lock you away.

The Interview Room at the Police Station

(*A close shot of Sadik's hand-cuffed wrists on the table. The camera pulls back as the door opens and Watt walks into the room. Two constables are standing just behind Sadik, close to his back. Watt sits down at the table opposite Sadik.*)

WATT	Sadik. (*Sadik lifts his head and looks at Watt.*) You know what we're going to talk about, don't you?

SADIK I tried to kill a man.

WATT That's right.

SADIK I hit him. (*He looks down at his hands on the table.*) I wanted to kill him. I hit his head. I saw the blood.

WATT Best if we start . . .

SADIK How could I do that? (*He stares desperately at Watt.*) How?

Barlow's office

(*Lowther is waiting for Barlow.*)

BARLOW Sorry I kept you hanging about, Lowther.

LOWTHER No, sir—no—that's perfectly all right. (*Barlow hangs up his coat.*) You got him out?

BARLOW Yes.

LOWTHER Nobody got hurt?

BARLOW No, as a matter of fact, they didn't. (*He walks across to his desk.*) We were lucky.

LOWTHER You certainly were.

BARLOW (*looking at some messages on his desk*) What's the latest on Wallace?

LOWTHER He's conscious again.

BARLOW He's going to pull through?

LOWTHER They won't go that far, but they seem pretty confident.

BARLOW Good. (*He looks up at Lowther.*) Well, now—what can I do for you?

LOWTHER Nothing, really—I suppose. Wanted to know you'd got him.

BARLOW He's downstairs. (*He sits down.*) Sergeant Watt's talking to him.

LOWTHER Is he? I doubt they'll have much to say to each other.
(*There is a pause.*)

BARLOW I hope you're wrong about that.

LOWTHER What?

BARLOW We don't know what really happened yet.

LOWTHER Plain enough, isn't it?

BARLOW That's a dangerous statement.

LOWTHER Wallace told you . . .

BARLOW When I spoke to him—for all of ten seconds, Lowther—he was in a state of semi-consciousness and all he told me was a name.

LOWTHER Well?

BARLOW We're talking about a charge of attempted murder.

LOWTHER That's right.

BARLOW I think we need to know a few details.

LOWTHER Sadik has a dozen court orders outstanding against him.

BARLOW Lowther . . .

LOWTHER (*interrupting*) No, you listen for a minute. I mean, I know what you think about us—all of us—in the warrant department.

BARLOW It's got nothing to do . . .

LOWTHER Couldn't call us police officers, could you!

BARLOW I don't know what . . .

LOWTHER (*belligerently*) My men have to go back there—go in amongst those savages, into their stinking holes, every day of their lives. It's not Wallace—not just Wallace I'm thinking about. There's all my men—and the next time . . .

(*There is a pause. Lowther turns away.*)

BARLOW I know how you feel.

LOWTHER (*abruptly*) Do you?

BARLOW (*coldly*) Yes, I do. (*After a pause.*) I still think we need to know a few more details.

The Interview Room

SADIK This man was banging—you know—on the door—and shouting.

WATT Yes?

SADIK I knew what he had come for.

WATT You opened the door?

SADIK He had come to take me away. You understand? Put me in jail. He said so.

WATT (*patiently*) You opened the door.

SADIK What would happen to my wife? My children. (*He pauses.*) He was shouting—and I thought—my home. This is my home.

Inside Sadik's room

(*It is later that evening. Mrs Lunt pulls down one of the coloured blankets which are hanging on the wall and drops it on to the floor. She moves slowly along the wall, takes hold of the next blanket, rips it down, and drops it on the floor beside the other. She steps away from the wall and looks round the room. The bed has been stripped, and the few personal belongings of the Sadiks piled on to the candlewick cover. Mrs Lunt bends down and picks up one of the coloured blankets. She pulls it along the floor to another, gathers that up, and takes them both along to the next. She rolls them up into a ball.)*

Barlow's office

(Nana is sitting in front of Barlow's desk. The children are sitting on chairs against the wall behind her.)

NANA   That is all then?

BARLOW   For the moment. Thank you.

NANA   You have my words. You have him safe—locked away—and that is the end.

BARLOW   Not entirely.

NANA   Yes. Entirely!

BARLOW   I haven't spoken to your husband yet.

NANA   You don't need to.

BARLOW   *(patiently)* Until I have . . .

NANA   *(interrupting)* You've seen him. He's black.

BARLOW   Mrs Sadik . . .

NANA   He had an axe in his hand. He was ready to kill you.

BARLOW   I don't think it helps . . .

NANA   *(vehemently)* You saw him. Surely—you don't need to speak to him. You know!

183

(*There is a pause.*)

BARLOW (*calmly*) Until I've spoken to him, I can't know, can I? I can't know anything.

NANA You would like to be different, perhaps—like to think you are—but you aren't.

Inside Z Victor One

(*The car is driving through the streets of Seaport by night.*)

JOCK 'Course, he was right!

FANCY I didn't reckon getting my hair parted. Not with a hatchet!

JOCK No more did I.

FANCY What you on about then?

JOCK Looking at him—when he walked out. Looking at his face.

FANCY I can't tell one from the other.

JOCK (*abruptly*) I don't know.

(*There is a pause.*)

FANCY Sulking, are you?

JOCK Don't be stupid!

FANCY What was it? Five on to one? or Barlow telling him lies?

JOCK Look, I know! He chopped Tom Wallace. He could've done the same to us.

FANCY He could.

JOCK It was—get him out—and—put him away! I know that. Only . . . (*Pause*) . . . looking at him—stood there. I wanted to know—why.

FANCY You should've asked him.

The Interview Room

(*Watt is studying the statement he has just written down.*)

SADIK I know clearly what I have done.

WATT What? (*He looks up from the written statement in front of him.*) Sorry, what did you say?

SADIK I know what I have done. I know it is wrong.

WATT Oh.

SADIK I know I must be punished.

WATT Yes. Just a minute, will you? I'll be finished looking through this . . .

SADIK It is right.

WATT Hmm. (*He looks down at the statement again.*)

SADIK I have never before . . . (*he shakes his head*) . . . never—the whole of my life—never—have I hit another man—struck out in fear—like an animal.

WATT You haven't got a job at the moment?
(*There is a pause.*)

SADIK No.

WATT Right. (*He stands up and picks up the statement.*) If you'll sign this.

Barlow's office

(*Isaacs has come as he promised. Barlow and Isaacs are sitting on either side of Barlow's desk. The desk light is the only light on at the moment and the room about them is shadowy.*)

ISAACS I saw Mr Sadik coming home. I saw him turn the corner.

BARLOW Yes.

ISAACS I am an old man. I have nothing better to do. I watch people as they come and go.

BARLOW You saw Sadik.

ISAACS An unhappy man. You've spoken to him?

BARLOW Briefly.

ISAACS Unhappy.

BARLOW Mr Isaacs, I'm sorry—but I haven't a great deal of time.

ISAACS I'm sorry. (*He puts up a hand.*) I'm sorry. I don't mean to waste your time.

BARLOW You understand . . .

ISAACS You're a busy man.

BARLOW One or two things to attend to.

ISAACS Mr Sadik is walking up the front steps, when the man calls to him.

BARLOW What man?

ISAACS The man—Wallace. The man Mr Sadik . . . (*He gestures and leaves the sentence unfinished.*)

BARLOW Well?

ISAACS I have seen Wallace before. He is well known in the neighbourhood.

BARLOW Did Sadik stop when Wallace called to him.

ISAACS He looked round. Yes—for a moment he stopped. Only for a moment. Wallace beckoned to him and said something else. I couldn't hear. From my window, it isn't possible to hear . . .

BARLOW What happened?

ISAACS Mr Sadik ran away.

BARLOW Into the house?

ISAACS Yes. Wallace ran after him. A few steps—and then he stopped.

BARLOW Why?

ISAACS Perhaps because he had no need to run. Where could Mr Sadik go? How could be escape?

BARLOW Wallace went into the house, after Sadik?

ISAACS Yes.

(*There is a pause.*)

BARLOW That's all?

ISAACS I think perhaps I've wasted your time after all.

BARLOW No. (*He sits back in his chair.*) Tell me, is there anyone else I can talk to? Anyone else knows Sadik? Might be able to help me?

ISAACS I don't know him! I mean, to recognise him—yes—walking in the street—to speak to him—no. I don't know him.

(*Isaacs sits forward as the camera moves in for a close-up.*)

I have sympathy for him.

The corridor leading to the cells

(*Sadik is being taken along the corridor towards the cell at the far end. He is walking between two constables, with a third walking ahead. The third constable unlocks the cell and pulls the door open.*

186

Sadik walks into the cell and the door is closed. The key is turned, the door is locked, and the three constables walk away. Suddenly, inside the cell, Sadik shouts a violent, wordless shout of pain.)

The landing outside Sadik's room

(Carrying the girl and holding the boy's hand, Nana climbs wearily up to the landing. She walks across to the door, lets go of the boy's hand and reaches for the door handle. She turns it and pushes. The door doesn't move. Nana rattles the handle and then turns it again. She pushes on the door. Still, it doesn't move. She steps away from the door and wakes the girl. She puts her down, gestures to the boy to go to comfort her. Nana takes hold of the door handle again and turns it violently, one way and then the other. She pushes at the door, but it doesn't open. Nana hits the door once with her fist and hurts herself. She looks at her hand. She holds it with the other. She lifts her head.)

NANA Adigun.

(The boy leaves the girl and runs to Nana. He hugs her round her legs. Cut to
A still photograph looking down the stairs at the empty first landing. Cut to
A still photograph looking across the empty second floor landing. Cut to
A still photograph looking along the empty hall, towards the door of Mrs Lunt's room.)

The corridor leading to the cells. Night

(We are looking along the empty corridor, towards the door of Sadik's cell. There is silence.)

Barlow's office

(*Barlow pours a cup of coffee for Lowther. Watt is sitting at the other desk.*)

LOWTHER   Thanks very much, sir.

BARLOW   Sugar. (*He gestures at the tray with coffee pot, cups, milk jug and sugar bowl on his desk.*) This bloke Wallace . . .

LOWTHER   Yes, sir.

BARLOW   (*pouring himself a cup of coffee*) What sort of fellow is he?
(*There is a pause. Barlow looks round at Lowther.*)

LOWTHER   (*carefully*) How d'you mean?

BARLOW   We'll get nowhere with you fencing about!

LOWTHER   We'll get nowhere without I know what're you're driving at. (*Slight pause.*) Sir.

BARLOW   He's got a difficult job. How does he do it?

LOWTHER   He does it well.

BARLOW   Does he—d'you reckon—does he enjoy it?

LOWTHER   Oh, yes. 'Course he does! He enjoys getting a chopper slammed into his head. Enjoys it no end.
(*After a pause, Barlow turns to look at Watt.*)

BARLOW   Cup of coffee, John?

WATT   Thank you, sir.

BARLOW   Help yourself. (*He sits down at his desk.*)

LOWTHER   What d'you expect me to say?

BARLOW   (*calmly*) I don't know.

LOWTHER   Like you say—Wallace has got a difficult job—unpleasant one. I shouldn't wonder there's plenty of people don't like him. Plenty of people don't like you, sir.

BARLOW   Plenty.

LOWTHER   All the same, if one of them took an axe to you, I should hope Sergeant Watt would think twice before saying it was your own fault, you brought it on yourself— 'Course the bloke did it was—well, coloured or something.

BARLOW   I'm not saying . . .

LOWTHER   Black, white or khaki—I don't give a damn! This fellow took an axe and near chopped Tom Wallace in half. One of my chaps. (*He bangs his hand on Barlow's desk.*) One of us! And you ask me—what sort of bloke is Tom!

BARLOW   I didn't say it was his own fault.

LOWTHER   I'll tell you—look, shall I tell you what sort of bloke he is? He's fifty-seven near enough. He's married. His wife's at the hospital! He's got two daughters, both married.

BARLOW   No, come on!

LOWTHER Twenty years on the beat, you know—before he packed it in.

BARLOW All right!

LOWTHER Now—he's got a dirty job and he does it well.

BARLOW Lowther! (*Pause*) You know what I'm talking about. You know damn well! I'm holding Sadik on attempted murder. All right?

LOWTHER Yes.

BARLOW Stands a fair chance of getting up to ten years on that. It's up to the judge—but you look at it. No provocation—anything up to ten.

LOWTHER You don't reckon he deserves it?

BARLOW (*angry*) See—that's where you're wrong. I mean, I know what's getting at you. You have to send your blokes back there tomorrow.

LOWTHER A dozen warrants in that area alone.

BARLOW You think I'm soft on this fellow Sadik—and your blokes'll have to take the rap for it. (*Pause*) Don't you?

LOWTHER I don't see why he should be treated different from anyone else!

BARLOW Who's treating him different!

LOWTHER You're making a special case of it.

BARLOW It is a special case! (*He stands up.*) Isn't it? For God's sake, isn't it? I mean—like you said—black, white or khaki—isn't it a special case? Here's a man—he's never hurt anyone the whole of his life. He's nothing against him.

LOWTHER What about the *court orders* out against him?

BARLOW Nothing for violence. Nothing for crime. Suddenly—one bright summer evening—he ups and clobbers a bloke with a hatchet. Come on—isn't that special?

LOWTHER You mean he's cracked?

BARLOW (*violently*) No, I don't mean . . .(*He stops and turns away from Lowther. He walks across to the window.*)

LOWTHER Well, then—what are you getting at?

BARLOW (*quietly*) I'm holding Sadik for attempted murder. It seems pretty certain now Wallace isn't going to die. So—do I let that charge stand, or—do I think about changing it? (*He turns to look at Lowther.*)

LOWTHER Change it to what?

BARLOW I thought—maybe—well, grievous bodily harm. Let him plead guilty . . .

LOWTHER What would he get?

BARLOW He could still get up to seven.

LOWTHER Hmmm.

BARLOW Yes. (*Pause*) Then, I thought—if the circumstances warrant it—I could do him for felonious wounding.

LOWTHER You could always turn him loose, too!

G

BARLOW   Right. I think you'd better get off home, don't you?

LOWTHER   He'll get no more than eighteen months.

BARLOW   Inspector Lowther—thank you for staying so long. . . . I'm sorry I had to keep you waiting.

LOWTHER   You know—do you know—there's only one way to keep them under? If you show you're soft—show weakness—d'you think they'll respect you for it? They'll laugh in your face.
        (*Barlow opens the door of his office.*)

BARLOW   I understand how you feel—about Wallace. I understand . . .

LOWTHER   Said that before, didn't you? (*He walks across to the door.*) I don't think you do. I don't think you've any idea.
        (*Lowther walks out, and Barlow shuts the door.*)

BARLOW   Asked for that, I suppose?

WATT   Well!

BARLOW   Yes. (*He walks back to his desk.*) Asking a bit much.

WATT   In the circumstances.

BARLOW   Aye. (*Sits down.*) What d'you know about Wallace?

WATT   He's right bad beggar, I'll tell you that.

BARLOW   Is he?

WATT   Known for it. I mean, he's one—all by himself—thank the Lord. But he's known for it.
        (*There is a pause.*)

BARLOW   See—Lowther thinks—he'll be telling everyone too! I'm soft on Sadik because he's coloured.

WATT   Hmm?

BARLOW   I'm not. I'm scared I'll be hard on him—double hard—'cause he's coloured. (*he sits back in his chair.*) Going up to get him, I was thinking . . . (*he shakes his head.*) 'And another of them!'—you know? Not fit to live among . . . (*he stands up and shrugs.*) Well.

WATT   Have you read his statement?

BARLOW   No, not yet. Why?

WATT   I think you should.

BARLOW   (*grimly*) I'll get round to it.

WATT   Give you a bit of a laugh.

BARLOW   (*abruptly*) What?

WATT   Well—depends on your sense of humour, I suppose.

BARLOW   What're you talking about?

WATT   Sadik's statement.

BARLOW   What about it?

WATT   One or two things—like—take you by surprise.

BARLOW   (*coldly*) Such as?

WATT   All those warrants out against him?

BARLOW Aye?

WATT Hire purchase—every single one.

BARLOW He gets the stuff—pays the deposit . . .

WATT (*interrupting*) Oh, no—it's better than that! His wife gets the stuff. These blokes come round to the door. They talk his missis into buying God knows what-all.

BARLOW Aye.

WATT He comes home. He's got no job.

BARLOW (*grimly*) No.

WATT (*quickly*) He's got a trade.

BARLOW Has he?

WATT Welder. Went to night school. No—matter of fact—soon as he got off the boat, there was an old fellow—he made him learn a trade.

BARLOW What sort of statement is this, John?

WATT Yes, well—you see—I was asking him the questions—you know—'What did you do then?'—and that. He was telling me the story of his life.

BARLOW Oh.

WATT West African. Crew boy on a boat. Got off in the docks . . .

BARLOW Learnt a trade!

WATT Last three places he went to—no colour bar, you understand—just—no colour, either.

BARLOW Hmm.

WATT So—there he is—near starving, out of work—and all this brand-new gear coming in. Obvious, isn't it?

BARLOW Flog it.

WATT Three vacuum cleaners. Two television sets. Five steam irons! Fast as she bought them—he sold them—and neither telling the other. Must have three-quarters the hire purchase firms in the country looking for them.

BARLOW Who's handling that side of the case?

WATT (*after a pause*) You took a statement from his missis, didn't you?

BARLOW I did. Yes. But it won't be much help. I mean, I didn't talk—like—housekeeping.

WATT I'll see her in the morning. (*Watt shuts the file in front of him.*) I should read it, sir. Might give you a laugh.

BARLOW I thought it was all—you know—over and done with! Got him out—and nobody hurt. (*Stands up.*) Over and done with!

WATT Aye.

BARLOW You do something—like—that bit clever and you think—'Right. That's it. That's me for the day. Where's the boozer'. By heck! (*He walks across the office.*) Quiet night. Nothing doing. Where am

191

I? Safe home with my feet up—watching a bit of telly? Oh, yes! Can't you see me?

WATT Better late than . . .

BARLOW Shut up! (*Barlow looks at Watt for a moment, and then, he grins.*) If you know what I mean?

WATT Aye.

BARLOW Should be easy! Fellow with a hatchet! You don't need to think twice. Get him out and lock him up. (*Pause*) There he is. Locked up.

WATT Likely asleep.

BARLOW Oh, aye—they can sleep anywhere. (*He looks at Watt again.*) You see? Double hard on him—'cause he's coloured. (*He turns away and stands, looking at the map.*) There must be something else happening.

A main street in Seaport

(*We are looking through the windscreen of Z Victor One, along the street at a bus shelter. A crowd of men are standing at the bus shelter, leaning on it, looking in, laughing and talking.*)

JOCK (*heard off screen*) What's going on there?

FANCY Have a look shall we?

(*Z Victor One moves forward towards the bus shelter.*)

JOCK Best send for the van.

FANCY No.

JOCK We'll never get that lot in here.

FANCY (*grimly*) We'll move 'em on.

(*Z Victor One stops. Jock opens the passenger's door and gets out.*)

The bus shelter

(*We hear the sound of the door slam. A couple of the men look round.*)

COLLINS Hey-up!

STEPHENS Jacks!

(*The men separate into two groups and through the groups it is possible to see Nana and the children, sitting on the bench in the shelter, pushed into the corner. Nana is sitting upright. The girl is stretched out with her head in her lap. The boy is sitting beside Nana.*)

COLLINS 'Evening, constable.

(*Jock and Fancy move forward between the men to Nana.*)

JOCK You all right?

STEPHENS She's all right.

COLLINS She's a bit of all right.

FANCY (*turning to speak to the men*) Don't get cheeky.

COLLINS Cheeky!

FANCY What're you doing here?

STEPHENS Ah.

COLLINS Waiting for a bus.

  (*There is a general chorus of agreement from the other men.*)

FANCY Last bus went near half an hour ago.

COLLINS We're waiting for the first bus.

FANCY You'll not wait here.

COLLINS If we fancy waiting, mate—we'll wait.

FANCY You won't! (*Fancy hauls Collins to his feet.*) They might. I'm not bothered about them. But you won't. 'Cause you'll be down the station.

STEPHENS Eh—no!

FANCY Shove off! (*He pushes Stephens away.*) The rest of you—shove off! (*A few of the drunks move away.*)

STEPHENS Look, what's he done?

FANCY All right. (*He turns his head and looks at Stephens.*) I'll take you too.

STEPHENS (*quickly*) No. Look . . . (*he steps back*) . . . I was only—like . . . (*he stops and turns away.*)

  (*Collins starts to move away.*)

FANCY (*violently*) Not you! Did I say anything to you?

COLLINS No.

FANCY Stand there! (*He points at the ground.*) There! D'you understand.

STEPHENS (*mournfully*) Hey, Stan . . .

FANCY Are you still here?

STEPHENS No.

  (*Stephens and the other men shuffle off, grumbling.*)

FANCY Right, now. (*He looks at Collins.*) What's your name?

COLLINS Stan Collins.

FANCY Where d'you live?

COLLINS Ninety-eight, Mather Road.

FANCY Making an nuisance of yourself, were you?

COLLINS No.

FANCY Bothering this lady.

COLLINS Talking to her.

FANCY (*looking round at Nana*) Was he bothering you?

NANA No.

COLLINS You see.

FANCY Shut up! (*Looking round at Collins*) Collins—you're drunk.

COLLINS I'm not.

FANCY Yes you are. Drunk. Damn near incapable.

COLLINS I am not.

FANCY Disorderly.

COLLINS Look, you're making . . .

FANCY Shall I knock him off? Drunk and disorderly.

COLLINS I'm not. Hey . . .(*He puts a hand on Fancy's shoulders*) . . .you're wrong.

FANCY Don't touch me! (*He turns round and catches hold of Collins*) What were you trying to do?

COLLINS Eh?

FANCY Were you trying to start a fight?

COLLINS No!

(*There is a pause.*)

FANCY Are you married?

COLLINS What?

FANCY Your wife'll wonder where've you got to.

COLLINS Oh.

FANCY Go home.

COLLINS Yes.

(*Fancy turns away and walks into the bus shelter.*)

FANCY Well, now. What about you?

JOCK Mrs Sadik.

FANCY That's it. You're . . . (*He looks at Jock, who nods*) What're you doing here?

NANA Shall I say—waiting for a bus?

JOCK That wouldn't be very clever.

NANA Perhaps not.

FANCY In a right old mess, weren't you?

NANA They would have gone away.

FANCY D'you reckon?

NANA They would've got bored.

JOCK What are you doing here?

NANA I'm trying to sleep.

FANCY You what!

JOCK What's happened?

NANA We have been thrown out of our room. I went home. The door was locked, my belongings . . . (*she shrugs*.) We have been thrown out.

JOCK You didn't reckon on staying here all night?

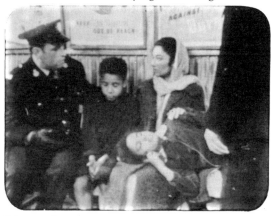

NANA Why not?

FANCY Well . . . (*he looks at the children. The boy stares back at him.*)

NANA They will be all right. They are with me.

JOCK Come on. (*He picks up one of the bundles of belongings.*)

NANA Where?

JOCK Back where you should be. (*Nana starts to laugh.*) Give us a hand, Fancy.

FANCY Aye, right. (*He rouses the child.*) What's so funny?

NANA They will not let us in.

(*The camera closes in on Nana as we cut to:*

Barlow's office

(*The telephone rings. Watt picks up the receiver.*)

WATT Sergeant Watt . . . Yes, Weir. What? . . . What're you going to do with them? . . . Oh. Right—see where that gets you. (*The other telephone rings and Watt picks up the receiver.*) Hang on.
(*Watt holds the receiver in his hands. Barlow pushes the door open and walks into the room.*)

WATT Locked the door on her? Did they? Hey, listen, that mate of yours. Watch him.

(*Barlow takes the other receiver out of Watt's hand.*)

BARLOW Chief Inspector here.

WATT If the door's locked—it's locked. If he kicks it in—he'll pay the damages. (*He puts the receiver down.*)

BARLOW Right, thanks. (*He puts the other receiver down.*) Sadik—gone beserk.

WATT (*looking up*) Hmm?

BARLOW Knocking the cell to pieces.

WATT What's he got? A pneumatic drill?

BARLOW (*gesturing to the other phone*) What was that?

WATT Weir.

BARLOW Oh.

WATT They found his wife.

BARLOW (*startled*) What?

WATT Sadik's wife—found her on the streets.

BARLOW Did they?

WATT She's been chucked out—bag and baggage.

The hall of the tenement

(*Nana and the children are just inside the front door. The boy is standing against Nana. The girl is sleeping on the floor, against Nana's feet.*
The camera shows us the boy and the girl as we hear Mrs Lunt's voice.)

MRS LUNT She can't come back here.

JOCK She's back.

MRS LUNT She can't stay.

FANCY She's staying.

MRS LUNT No, she isn't.

FANCY Get up there and open that flaming door.

MRS LUNT No.

JOCK Mrs Lunt ...

MRS LUNT Go on! Get out the lot of you! Get out!

(*Jock and Fancy are standing toe to toe with Mrs Lunt at the bottom of the stairs.*)

JOCK Unlock that door.

MRS LUNT No.

FANCY I'll go up there. I'll kick it in.

MRS LUNT No, you won't. (*There is a pause. Then she concludes triumphantly.*) No, you won't.

(*Fancy looks at Jock.*)

JOCK You can't leave them sleep on the streets?

MRS LUNT It's where they belong. Isn't it? Where they belong.

FANCY (*grimly*) You open that door, missis ...

196

MRS LUNT (*quickly*) I can't. No. I can't. If I wanted to—and I don't. If I did—landlord's took the key.

FANCY No, he hasn't.

MRS LUNT Came here this evening—himself. Said—'Mrs Lunt—get those things out of that room'—and I did—and he locked it—when I had.

FANCY You're lying.

JOCK You've got a spare key.

MRS LUNT No, I haven't.

FANCY You must have.

MRS LUNT No.

FANCY Keep it in your room do you?

MRS LUNT You won't go in there.

JOCK Come on—give them house room.

MRS LUNT No.

FANCY By heck!

(*Fancy walks across the hall and knocks on the door facing the bottom of the stairs.*)

MRS LUNT It's nothing to do with me. What the landlord says—that's what I do.

JOCK Is it?

(*Fancy knocks again.*)

MRS LUNT They won't answer.

FANCY Won't they? (*He knocks again.*)

MRS LUNT It's after midnight.

JOCK What're you doing?

FANCY They'll give her a room—just tonight.

(*Nana laughs.*)

MRS LUNT (*turning on Nana*) Go on! Walk the streets. That's what you're good for. They've put him away. They'll put you away too—soon enough. Put you all away. That's it. Lock you up—or send you back—where you came from. Bloody savages.

JOCK Come on, Fancy.

FANCY Aye.

(*Jock and Fancy turn away.*)

MRS LUNT (*straight to Nana*) You'll never see him again. They've got him now. Locked him up. You'll never see him again.

The corridor leading to the cells

(*Barlow and a policeman are going towards Sadik's cell. The constable unlocks the door and Barlow pulls it open. We see Sadik over Barlow's shoulder.*)

Inside the cell

(*Sadik is sitting in the corner of the cell. He has torn the blankets to pieces and scattered them round the cell. His forehead is bleeding where he has smashed it against the wall. Barlow steps into the cell and shuts the door behind him. Sadik looks up at him, his eyes full of tears, and shakes his head.*)

Barlow's office. Night

(*Watt is speaking on the telephone.*)

WATT Phone him in the morning, sir. He's a bit busy just now. No, I shouldn't worry. I'm sure he understood.

(*The other telephone rings.*)

Inspector Lowther, I'm sorry—the other phone's ringing . . . Yes, I'll tell him you called . . .Yes. (*He picks up the other receiver.*) Yes, I will. (*He puts the first receiver down.*) Hallo . . . Oh, yes, Weir? . . . Did she? What're you going to do with them now? . . . No. Well, you can't put them back, can you? . . . I said you can't, didn't I? Here—bring them in. I'll see what I can find for them. (*He puts down the receiver.*)

Inside Z Victor One

(*Jock pulls open the passenger's door and gets into the car, next to Fancy. He looks over the back of the seat at Nana and the children who are now in the car.*)

JOCK We'll take you to the station.

FANCY Oh, aye?

JOCK I've spoken to Sergeant Watt. He'll find you somewhere.

NANA Somewhere together.

JOCK He'll do his best.

(*The boy leans towards Nana and whispers in her ear.*)

NANA He says—will it be with his father?

Inside the cell

(*Sadik is still sitting against the wall, in the corner. Barlow is sitting on the bench-bed.*)

SADIK I am most frightened of myself. I find this anger in me—hatred. Deep in me—and I am afraid of it. The man—hunted me—shouted at me—cursed me. Not the first man to curse—but he hunted me. Like an animal—and I turned—like an animal. (*He looks up at Barlow.*) I have heard people call us animals—and laughed. Never

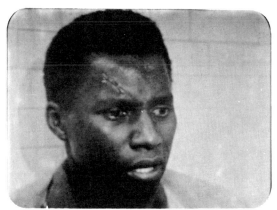

before have I found that—found—the animal. The men outside the door—after . . . I would have hurt them too. I would have killed them had they broken their way into my home. I would have tried to kill them. It frightens me to think . . . (*He shudders.*) The fear—closes round me—like these walls . . . (*He touches the wall behind him.*) . . . close round. Despair. And then . . . (*He picks up a shred of a blanket and looks at it, lying across his hand.*) Am I so different? Nana says—you're different, be different. Do not be like them. (*He looks at Barlow.*) Am I so different? Is she right?

The Interview Room

(*Nana is sitting by the table. The girl is sitting with her head asleep on the table. The boy is sitting on the other chair, with his head on his arms, also asleep.*)

Barlow's office. Night

WATT It's the best I can do.

JOCK She wants to keep them all together.

WATT That's her bad luck.

JOCK Surely, it's not so difficult . . .

WATT All right, Weir! I'll tell you what. (*He picks up the receiver and pushes it at Jock.*) There's the phone. You get on to all your friends— all the homes for waifs and strays, fallen women and unmarried mothers—city, county and national—go on. See what you can do! (*There is a pause.*)

JOCK I'm sorry.

WATT You've got the addresses? (*He puts the receiver down again.*)

JOCK Yes, sarge.

WATT Get off then. . . .
(*The door opens and Barlow walks in.*)
Let's hear no more about it.

JOCK No, sarge.
(*Barlow holds the door and watches Jock as he walks out of the office. Barlow shuts the door.*)

BARLOW What was that?

WATT (*abruptly*) Nothing.
(*He turns and walks back to the other desk.*)

BARLOW Oh.

WATT Got him quietened down, have you? (*He sits down.*)

BARLOW Quietened himself down.

WATT Did he?

BARLOW Aye. (*He walks across to his desk and stands, looking down at it.*)

WATT Nothing new.

BARLOW Mix-up! Muddle! Mess! That's what it is.

WATT Sir?

BARLOW Should never have started thinking about it.

WATT No sir.

BARLOW He's violent. (*He picks up a memo and drops it into his in-tray.*) Put him there. He's black. (*He picks up another memo and drops it into his in-tray.*) Put him there. He's a thief. (*He picks up a pamphlet and glances at the cover for a moment.*) Put him there. (*He drops the pamphlet on top of the memos.*) He half kills a police officer . . . (*He pulls out his key ring.*) . . . 'in the execution of his duty'. That's clear enough. (*He locks the centre drawer of his desk.*) And all the time—nagging at you—'you know why he did it—come on—take the easy way—he did it—'cause he's coloured'. (*He walks across and takes his hat off the hat stand.*) I think I'll go home.

WATT Oh, yes, sir. (*He stands up and walks across to help Barlow put his coat on.*) It's not easy.

BARLOW (*abruptly*) No, it isn't. If it was easy, we'd know what to do about it. (*He shrugs himself into his coat.*) What was all that? You—and Weir?

WATT Sadik's wife—and children.

BARLOW What about them?

WATT I found them somewhere to sleep the night.

BARLOW Good.

WATT Smith and Weir're dropping them off.

BARLOW Ah. (*He opens the door.*)

WATT He was saying—they wanted to keep together.

BARLOW That's their bad luck.

(*Barlow walks out and shuts the door.*)

Inside Z Victor One

(*Fancy puts on the brake and turns off the engine. Jock opens the door and gets out. He walks back and opens the back door.*)

FANCY Here we are then.

(*Nana moves across and starts to get out.*)

FANCY Crikey!

NANA (*still in the car, stopping to look back at Fancy*) I'm sorry. Did you say something?

FANCY No.

NANA (*after a pause*) You were expecting me to say 'Thank you'?

FANCY I said nothing.

NANA Why should I thank you? What have you done? Taken my children

from me.

FANCY If it wasn't for us. . .

NANA You've done no more than your duty—as policemen. Had you been men—men like those men—jeering at me—ordinary men—would you have done as much?

FANCY Look, go on—buck up, will you?

NANA If I were like you perhaps I would say 'Thank you'—and not mean it, because I have nothing to thank you for. I am not like you. We are not like you. We are like ourselves.

JOCK Come on.

NANA When you help me because I am half-Indian, half-African—and you are a man—a white man—then, perhaps—I will thank you.

JOCK Mrs Sadik.

NANA Yes. I am coming.

(She swings her legs out of the car and pulls the bundle of belongings after her.)

JOCK Here. Let me. . .

NANA No. *(She pulls the bundle out of the car and stands up.)* Will I be able to see my children in the morning?

JOCK Yes, of course. Look . . .

NANA When?

JOCK Whenever you like. No one's going to keep them away from you.

NANA You have the addresses?

JOCK Oh, yes. Here.

FANCY Come on, Jock.

NANA Thank you. *(Jock shuts the back door.)* When can I see my husband?

FANCY See him in court. Ten-thirty in the morning.

(There is a pause, and then we cut to:

The cell

(Sadik is sitting on the bench-bed staring into space.)

A small dormitory room in a council home

(Looking across the room, at the boy in bed, staring into space. As his eyes move, cut to:)

Inside Z Victor One
(Jock and Fancy are sitting silently in the car, without moving.)

A large dormitory room in a council home
A medium close-up of the girl in bed, staring into space.

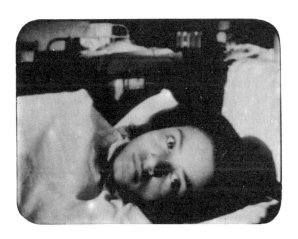

Inside Z Victor One

ANN *(sharply)* BD to Z Victor One.
(Jock snaps almost to attention as he reaches for the W/T receiver.)
JOCK Z Victor One.
ANN Z Victor One—Smithson's Warehouse, Stanley Road, Seaport Alarm Call.
(Fancy starts the engine.)
JOCK Z Victor One—wilco.
FANCY Thank God for that!

Nana's Room

(*A small, sparsely furnished room in a private home. Nana is sitting on the edge of the bed.*)

NANA (*suddenly*) I would like to cry.

A street in Seaport

(*We are looking down at the car as it swings away from the curb and drives fast along the street, into the darkness.*
The street fades out, and we see for a moment the empty corridor leading to the cells.)

Some technical words used in television scripts

The plays in this book were written for production in a television studio obviously. The authors therefore thought about what the camera could photograph, and wrote their plays with the camera in mind. Some of the camera instructions have been left in the scripts as printed here (but not all of them). The following words have been used to indicate some of the main camera and editing terms:

CUT The sudden change from one picture to another. This is done by switching from one camera to a second camera which is picking up a different picture or a different view of the same picture. On film (which is used for many of the exterior scenes) a CUT is done by actually cutting and rejoining lengths of film taken by the same camera from different angles.

FADE The picture grows dimmer and leaves the screen completely.

MIX One picture is FADED from the screen at the same time as a second picture is FADED in. For a moment, then, the two pictures are 'mixed' on the screen.

PAN Describes the movement of the camera swivelling whilst remaining in the same base position. (So called because the camera gives, so to speak, a 'panoramic' view.)

SHOT The name for the angle or viewpoint given to the camera. A CLOSE SHOT, for instance, is taken with the camera close to the person or object being shot.

TRACK An alternative type of movement when the whole camera (mounted on wheels) moves with the character it is following, either forwards and backwards, or sideways.

ZOOM A quick focusing down from a broad distant shot to a narrow close shot. (This is done by a zoom lens which can be adjusted to a different focus whilst actually taking its picture.)

Questions for Discussion

A Quiet Night

1 What are the first reactions of the various members of the police on duty to the news of a drunk at the pub?

2 What, in fact, is Regan on about when he says: 'These days, no idea' (page 39)?

3 Do Graham and Lynch agree about how Regan ought to be dealt with?

4 Why does the author show us the girl on duty in the information room tidying her things up (page 63)?

5 Look at the way each of the policemen take the news of Nicholson's row with his wife: Graham, Lynch, Blackitt, Watt. Can you see any differences? Would a woman have reacted in any of these ways? (When you are thinking about Watt's remarks on page 54, it is worth knowing that Watt's wife left him some years ago according to other episodes in the series.)

6 A 'quiet night' is unexpected by the men on duty. How do they behave? Do they all react to the lack of excitement in the same way?

7 Whose fault was it that Regan died, or couldn't it have been helped?

Window Dressing

1 What impression of Plimmer and Greenhalgh do we get from the first sequence on the roof? What differences do we notice between them?

2 What effect does Mercer's 'outburst' (page 80) have on Watt? On Greenhalgh?

3 When Watt questions Mrs Greenhalgh we hear about Terry's stealing and his parents' reaction to the theft. How do you think his parents ought to have acted when they discovered the theft?

4 Why does Aspin leave the room so quickly when he sees

Watt waiting outside (page 91)?

5 On first reading, the conversation between Baker and Graham on page 91 might well seem pointless. Why, then, has the author included this in the play?

6 What is Aspin getting at when he talks about 'isolation' (page 97)?

7 What do you think of the way; Aspin makes contact with Greenhalgh and gets talking to him at the baths (pages 101–105)?

8 What connection with the main story has the incident with Carroll and Sampson?

9 Which do you feel most sympathy for in the argument on pages 108 and 109, Barlow or Watt?

10 Barlow is the 'boss', and Barlow's instructions are obeyed. What is gained by them? What is lost by them?

11 The play ends with Watt phoning to apologise to Mercer. Looking back over the story, what are your feelings about Mercer? Does he behave reasonably?

12 The author probably had more than one reason for choosing the title for this play: *Window Dressing*. What do you think his reasons were?

Running Milligan

1 Milligan is a 'criminal'. What sort of character do we expect a criminal to have, and how do we expect a criminal to behave? How do these expectations compare with the impression that we have of Milligan by the end of his first meeting with Cath?

2 What is it that Barlow and Blackitt are disagreeing about on page 118–119? Is Barlow lacking ordinary human sympathy for a man whose wife has died?

3 Mr Fletcher cannot understand the behaviour of his daughter, Cath. Why is this? Which of the two do you think is right?

4 What is Milly's opinion of Milligan?

5 What reason does Barlow think that Milligan had for visiting the Ganger?

6 At the end of the story Alderman Wilson comes face-to-face with Milligan. Earlier he said that he knows Milligan's 'sort':

'Pretty low type.' How well does Alderman Wilson understand Milligan?

7 Why does the author choose to actually show us one of the police dogs when the police surround the old waiting room at the end?

8 Early in the play Barlow says that parole is 'Well meant, but ridiculous'. By the end of the play, do we agree or disagree with this?

9 Milligan has caused a great deal of trouble, taking police time from other jobs, and, as Barlow points out: 'One man like Milligan can destroy the happiness of a whole family.' At the end of the story Milligan says: 'It wasn't nobody's fault, really it wasn't.' How much blame for Milligan's failures can we place on him? If he himself is not entirely to blame, can we then criticise anyone else? What can and should the community do about someone like Milligan?

A Place of Safety

1 As we watch the attack on Wallace and the arrival of the police we are given a few glimpses of life in this block of tenement flats. What is your impression of what it would be like to live there?

2 Why does Barlow question Mrs Lunt about whether Sadik is right- or left-handed? What does this conversation tell us about both Barlow and Mrs Lunt?

3 'Treat them like animals, and you get animals to deal with!' says Barlow (page 176). What is the difference in approach between Fancy and Jock and Barlow when they reach the house? What is your opinion of Barlow's method of getting Sadik?

4 Mrs Lunt thinks all coloured people are dangerous ('I read where one of them blackies did his whole family in') and that the police are not to be trusted. Do people like Mrs Lunt exist, or is her character hopelessly exaggerated by the writer? If you think that there are people like her, what do you think makes them so prejudiced?

5 Why does the writer bring Isaacs into the story?

6 What is Lowther's attitude towards the incident and how it should be dealt with?

7 What are Sadik's feelings about the crime that he has committed?

8 What are Nana and Fancy arguing about on page 201–202?

9 Looking back can you see any difference between Jock and Fancy in this play?

10 Sadik is 'one of them blackies'. This fact affects everyone in the play. Compare how the various characters react to his colour.

11 What does the future hold for the Sadik family?

General

1 Describe the occasions shown in these plays when the feelings of the policemen as *people* conflict with their duties as *police*?

2 Do you consider that any of the policemen shown in these plays acted wrongly?

3 What difficulties are we shown that make the job of the police in these stories more awkward than it need be?

4 We are shown a number of characters who have done wrong, who have committed a 'crime'. Do we feel sympathy for any of these people?

5 Very often there seems to be a conflict between the rule which has to be laid down for everybody and a particular case which seems to need unusual treatment. In *Window Dressing*, for instance, the Probation Officer says: 'It's an unusual case.' And Watt, meaning that nothing unusual can be done, replies: 'Well, they all are.' A similar disagreement comes in the final play. Lowther argues with Barlow, saying: 'You're making a special case of it!' And Barlow retorts: 'It *is* a special case, isn't it?'

Can any general rules be made? Must all the unusual sides, to an individual case be pushed aside for the sake of keeping to the general rule for the general good?

Use the incidents in the four plays to discuss this question.

6 Remembering that these are plays for *television*, find examples of each of the following that you consider make very important contributions to one of the plays:

(a) A Close-Up;

(b) A sequence of pictures without any dialogue;

(c) Cutting from one scene to another.

The Authors

Keith Dewhurst

Keith Dewhurst was born in Oldham in 1931; he went to Rydal School, Colwyn Bay, and then on to Cambridge University. He·worked for a time in a cotton mill, and later was for some time a reporter with Kemsley Newspapers in Manchester. During much of this time he was travelling reporter with the Manchester United football team, and covered the 1958 world cup with them. Since 1959 he has been a freelance television writer. He has written other *Z Cars* plays, including *Birds of the Air*, and a play for schools television specially commissioned by the BBC: *The Life of Karen Gillhooly*. His first stage play *Rafferty's Chant* was produced at the Mermaid Theatre, London, in 1967.

Ronald Eyre

Ronald Eyre was born in Yorkshire (the setting of *The Victim* which is included in *Conflicting Generations* in this series) in 1929. After serving in the Air Force he went to University College, Oxford, where he was secretary of the Oxford University Dramatic Society, acting in many Oxford productions and making a tour of the USA. After Oxford, Ronald Eyre became an English teacher, first at Queen Elizabeth Grammar School, Blackburn, and then at Bromsgrove School.

In 1956 he joined the BBC schools television department as a drama producer, and for eight years directed the schools drama programmes, which included plays as varied as *The Caucasian Chalk Circle, Julius Caesar, The Queen and The Rebels*, and *The Victim*, which he wrote especially for this series. Towards the end of this time, Ronald Eyre directed a number of plays for the normal evening programmes, including *The Fire Raisers* and *As You Like It*, and an episode for the *Z Cars* series, which he wrote himself, *Window Dressing*. So far he has written six television plays, one of which, *A Crack in the Ice*, he later adapted for the stage and it was successfully produced at the Birmingham Repertory Theatre. More recently Ronald Eyre has also directed a number of plays in the theatre, including a widely praised production of Shaw's *Widower's Houses*.

John Hopkins

John Hopkins went to Cambridge University before working for BBC radio. He has written more for television than for any other medium. He wrote fifty-three of the episodes for the first run of the BBC's *Z Cars* series, and edited many more. For his work on this series he won the Screenwriters Guild Award for the best series work two years running. His full-length plays for television include *A Game – Like – Only A Game* (included in *Conflicting Generations* in this series), *Horror of Darkness*, and *Fable*. He also wrote the libretto for a television opera which the BBC commissioned in 1967. John Hopkins has written the scripts for a number of films, including the James Bond film *Thunderball*, *Funeral in Berlin*, and *Night of the Short Knives*. In 1966 his most ambitious television play was screened: *Talking to a Stranger*. This was a quartet of plays, each looking at the same events from a different point of view.

Alan Plater

Alan Plater started to write whilst still in his teens. He was born in Jarrow-on-Tyne, but his family moved to Hull when he was three. When he left Kingston High School, Hull, he went to King's College, Newcastle, to study architecture, which he saw, as he puts it, as a 'respectable alternative to ivory towers'. After two years in an architect's office in Hull ('the only real job I've ever had'), he became a full-time writer when his first play, the *Smoke Zone*, was broadcast on the radio in 1961.

Sound radio gave him his first opportunities, and eight of his plays have been produced including *Mating Season* (included in the volume *Worth a Hearing*, in Blackie's *Student Drama* series). Alan Plater has written an even larger number of plays for television, including *A Smashing Day*, *So-Long Charlie*, and the *Nutter*. The *Z Cars* series was of especial interest to him, and the script in this volume was one of eighteen which he wrote for the series.

The live theatre, particularly when closely attached to a particular region, interests Alan Plater most. The Victoria Theatre, Stoke-on-Trent has produced many of his stage plays, including *Ted's Cathederal*. This theatre has grown out of *local* interest, and Alan Plater feels strongly that the arts flourish most valuably in a regional setting so that each region needs an Arts Centre. He is deeply involved in schemes for such a centre in his own city, Hull.

An Introduction for Teachers

Staple fodder of bookstall and bedside, the detective story has been the despair of the teacher of English, not least because of the addiction of so many of the 'educated', and the gracing of the reading and even the writing of detective stories by so many of the 'distinguished'. Inevitably such stories swell the piles of school 'readers' for, the teacher must feel, surely the appeal of the detective story can be exploited when faced with the difficulty, for difficulty it will always remain, of finding books that have a strong appeal in the middle years of the secondary school.

But the gleanings have been sad, for the heyday of the detective story yielded, it will surely be agreed, little more than empty elegance of language in the service of pointless ingenuity of plot. The heyday of such stories has probably passed, but the sex-and-violence thrillers that surreptitiously go the rounds in schools have even less to offer as points of contact between the crazes of out-of-school reading and the real exploration of literature.

Such a point of contact has, however, been found in the popularity of the plays in the *Z Cars* series. In the three years and some one hundred and seventy episodes of its first screen run, the *Z Cars* series attracted a wider and more varied range of viewers than most programmes. Significantly teacher and taught found a common meeting point in the weekly play. Many teachers of English reported that the *Z Cars* plays were enjoyed by pupils as part of the normal, unsponsored, evening's entertainment of the home, and at the same time were real dramas that would spark off sharp discussion of 'theme' and 'form', though not in those terms, in class the next day. When the series ended, the *Radio Times* printed a letter from one teacher that was typical of the response of many: 'It is a pity that the series cannot continue for the sake of its value to schools.'

What was this value? Firstly, it seems to me to grow from

213

the fact that in these plays crime is being written about not for the thrill of 'who dun' it?', but for the exploration of *why*, and also, for here is the significant underlying theme of this collection, what *we*—the police, the public, the audience—feel towards 'who dun' it'. Jock, in *A Place of Safety*, could be speaking for the whole collection of plays when he says:

'Only . . . looking at him—stood there, I wanted to know—why.'

Or Aspin, in *Window Dressing*, when he argues:

'You can't just pick out the criminal bits and forget the rest.'

The second point is that, unlike the detective story of tradition, we are not asked to identify ourselves with a detective superman of immense cleverness, romantic appeal, and possibly physical strength. As we read these plays, we realise that the policemen portrayed are desperately limited people. (What is there in their training and selection to make them otherwise?) There are variations: Jock's reaction to Nana's plight and Sadik's violence reveals more humanity than Fancy's for instance. Yet, despite their tenacity, skill, and sometimes wit, we see that these men are trained to 'deal with' and to 'handle' situations and people, not to 'feel for' or 'sympathise with'. It would be a poor English lesson that did not explore these personal inadequacies—and a poor lesson that did not discover that these are not inadequacies of 'the police', but of *people* who happen to be policemen, and because they are policemen find human predicament a daily routine that cannot be avoided.

In making this point, we find the third appeal that the plays have to the teacher, one that comes from what is perhaps the major theme of these four plays, indeed of the whole series. In a valedictory article to the final programme printed in the *Radio Times*, a former Detective Chief Superintendent declared of the series: 'The purpose was to depict the "ordinary policeman" going about his everyday work.' This may have been so, but it seems that, consciously or not, a more interesting purpose lay behind many of the episodes, a purpose that concerned the community rather than just the police: by recruiting an organised and paid 'police', the community is, necessarily perhaps, passing the buck. When, for instance, Graham and Baker in *Window Dressing* bundle the young Greenhalgh, 'like an animal' into the car, we are shrugging onto uniformed shoulders a human problem which as individuals we have no time for, and as a community we have no understanding of.

It is clear how this third theme of the responsibility of the community links with the previous one of the limitations of many of the police in the plays. Watt states this in his explosion against Barlow in *Window Dressing*:

WATT Police work is detecting crime?

BARLOW Yes.

WATT Finding suspects, breaking 'em down, running 'em in?

BARLOW Yes.

WATT At high speed?

BARLOW At top speed?

WATT And there's nothing more to it?

BARLOW In this case, nothing.

WATT Then if that's all, it's a job for barbarians.

BARLOW (*very deliberately*) Then you're a sergeant barbarian, Watt. That's not bad. And I'm an inspector barbarian. That's even better. Folk must take us as they find us.

In these plays, then, the old appeal of the crime story is used by the writers for their own ends and thereby given new point. Schools can use these scripts as classroom reading with three related but separate functions:

☐ play-reading of effective drama;
☐ the study of source material for work in television appreciation;
☐ the discussion of concrete situation and characters for the understanding of contemporary social themes.

Z Cars as plays

While the first series was running public discussion chewed over two worries: Was it right for viewers to see the police in something other than an idealised role, 'eating disgustingly', for instance, smoking on duty, or having a flutter on the horses? Secondly, should viewers be shown so much violence? The general run of the fourteen million viewers were more concerned, perhaps, with the foibles of the recurrent characters. Looking back, though, what is more important is that the series was not churned out by a team of hacks but was attractive to a wide variety of real writers who often found the format a suitable one within which they could write *plays* that interested them. The feeling of personal involvement that comes through in the writing of these scripts is unexpected in purely 'series' writing.

A short play of the length of these should have the virtues of a short story: direct observation pointed to a relevant sense of life. Looked at as plays, these scripts will be seen to have a quality of honest observation. (The casebook material on which many were based was clearly helpful, although other uses of the same type of material, in various *Z Cars* books, reminds us that it is not the material itself but the treatment that makes for honesty.) The plays are almost always economical, indeed the dialogue may seem thin compared with a stage play. However it is always suitable for its dramatic function at each point in the play, and can rise to an expressive naturalism for key moments, such as Milligan's fumbling conversation with his sister-in-law, Cath.

The characters, it is true, are revealed rather than explored, but the central characters are real, and are revealed with the ear and eye of the writer sensitive to the interaction of people and to social tension.

It will be found that the scripts read well in the classroom, and can even, with slight adaptations, be recorded as 'radio' plays. At other times, the most effective classroom technique is for the play as a whole to be read silently, perhaps for homework, and certain of the major confrontations re-read aloud in class. The texts have been edited so that they can be easily and coherently read straight through, almost as a short story, with technicalities (as is explained later) kept to a minimum. However the scripts are first read, class discussion afterwards should bring out the characters and themes, and how the writers have chosen to reveal these in dramatic terms.

Z Cars for television appreciation

Although in the late teens boys and girls habitually escape from the television domination of the home, it is obvious that television is the major cultural experience of the nation, and will continually be so for some years. The Newsom report (*Half Our Future*, HMSO, 1963) confirmed the responsibility of schools for education in television appreciation:

> 'The culture provided by all the mass media, but particularly by film and television, represents the most significant environmental factor that teachers have to take into account.... The media help to define aspirations and they offer roles and models. They not only supply needs (and create them) but may influence attitudes and values. Little as yet has been effectively undertaken in schools in the way of offering some counterbalancing assistance. We need to train children to look critically and discriminate between what is good and bad in what they see.' (para. 475)

Many schools, of course, are attempting to do just this, but the difficulty is that television is a transitory and home-based medium. Very little material is available for use in the classroom, and, surprising as it may seem there are very few school edition of television plays (see, for instance, *Conflicting Generations*—five television plays edited by the present writer, Longmans, Green 1967). (Certain programmes are available on film from the British Film Institute, 81 Dean Street, London W.1, and a great deal of advice is available to members of The Society for Education in Film and Television, 34 Second Avenue, London E.17.)

It is certainly unrealistic to discuss television drama without also reading some actual scripts. The contribution of the writer to the programme is possibly not very obvious to the ordinary viewer, and the realisation of the importance of the script helps the pupil to apply more objective standards of

judgement to the actual content and quality of the programme as a play.

The scripts printed here have been edited from the re-
hearsal and camera scripts used in making the actual
programmes. Almost all the detailed camera instructions
have had to be ommitted, but in the context of television
appreciation it was obviously important to retain the feel of
a presentation in terms of cameras and screen. Therefore
from time to time, particularly at key moments, directions
for specific camera shots have been included. The editing is
deliberately inconsistent: it is hoped that there are sufficient
of these references to make the reader think of the small-
screen presentation, but not so many as to hinder continuous
reading.

Any teacher who has attempted to discuss television in
school will know of the huge temptation to wander too freely
into the fields of technical backroom details. In fact most
of the schoolbook presentation of television is of the 'How it
is done' variety. To some extent, admittedly, a working
knowledge of the technicalities is necessary to the teacher:
at any rate a knowledge of the possibilities and disadvantages
of the medium. But it is not television appreciation simply to
tell about how television works, as is so often done. What
matters is to deepen the enjoyment and sharpen the appreciation of content and performance.

The teacher has to decide which technical features will
help and which are irrelevant to this. For instance, whether
a scene is filmed or shot in the studio has been eliminated
from these scripts because the knowledge does not help our
appreciation. On the other hand, the attention of pupils
should be drawn to such points as the advantages and disadvantages of the series format which so dominates all
broadcasting; the use of particular camera angles to point
a scene (for instance, why have a close-up of Blackitt, who
is the listener, when Wilson remarks about Milligan: 'I know
them, inside out!'?); the amount that can be expressed by
the silent projection of single shots (the undrunk cups of tea
in *A Quiet Night*, for instance); or the editing which produces

ironic comment by juxtaposition (the shot of the ambulance men carrying out Tim Regan, for instance, immediately followed by the girl in the Information Room tidying away her things); or the possibility that television allows of the writer breaking off a scene at the thematically appropriate moment with no need to round off the incident and get the characters off stage.

These, and many more, are features of television that are helpful to a television appreciation course, and these four scripts are suitable for a real study of what television is about.

Z Cars and the social themes

The Schools Council's Working Paper No. 2, *Raising the School Leaving Age* (HMSO, 1965), confirmed and amplified the theme of the Newsom report that work at the senior end of a secondary school should be 'outgoing'. Teachers in Social Studies, Religious Education, History, and English are increasingly using their specialist approaches to help classes towards an understanding of social questions of today. This work is not easy. The Newsom report quoted the comment of a pupil:

'But when they say to you "What do you think?" well, there's nothing to say and you begin to dread discussion lesson in case he asks you for your opinion and you don't know anything about the subject.'

This same pupil, who has, for example, no discussable opinion on 'The problems of the elderly' would have forceful enough opinions on Tim Regan's plight. As Newsom goes on: 'They need lively presentation in terms of real people and events, if they are not to seem arid abstractions to most boys and girls.' (para. 213)

By the vivid dramatic presentation in these four plays we can talk not about 'arid abstractions' but about Freddie Milligan, Tim Regan, Adigun Sadik, and Terry Greenhalgh. One is reminded in this linking of the fictitious with the factual of Lawrence's remark: 'Art has two great functions. First, it provides an emotional experience. And then, if we have the

219

courage of our own feelings, it becomes a mine of practical truth.'

Early postwar television attempted a number of 'dramatised documentaries'. Worthy efforts they were, but the well-meaning documentary did not allow the dramatist scope, and therefore, paradoxically, they were less effective as documentary. Although these plays have the broader implications of documentary, they are centred on closely observed individuals. The teacher of social studies will find, in Lawrence's words, 'a mine of practical truth' on the 'subjects' of the weak criminal, rebellious youth, the old and the lonely, colour problems, and so on, from pupils who have reacted to the 'emotional experience' presented in these plays.

Here for classroom reading and discussion is what might be regarded as an episodic drama made up of four dramatic studies of our society, illustrated by both the official agents (the police, the probation officer) and the representatives of us all (Mr Preston, Mercer, Cath, Mrs Lunt), which moulds and must ultimately take responsibility for the social misfits that are at the centre of the drama.